JEW

Jonathan Rosen, General Editor

Jewish Encounters is a collaboration between Schocken and Nextbook, a project devoted to the promotion of Jewish literature, culture, and ideas.

PUBLISHED

FORTHCOMING

Benjamin Disraeli

ADAM KIRSCH

BENJAMIN DISRAELI

NEXTBOOK · SCHOCKEN · NEW YORK

Schocken Books and colophon are registered trademarks of
Random House, Inc.

Library of Congress Cataloging-in-Publication Data
Kirsch, Adam, [date]
   Benjamin Disraeli / Adam Kirsch.
         p. cm. — (Jewish encounters)
   ISBN 978-0-8052-4249-2
   1. Disraeli, Benjamin, Earl of Beaconsfield, 1804–1881.
2. Great Britain—Politics and government—1837–1901.
3. Prime ministers—Great Britain—Biography.   4. Jews—
Great Britain—Biography.   I. Title.
                  DA564.B3K57   2008
                  941.081092—dc22
                        [B]

                                         2008001628

                  www.schocken.com
         Printed in the United States of America
                     First Edition
                  2 4 6 8 9 7 5 3 1

For my father, Jonathan, and my son, Charles

CONTENTS

INTRODUCTION

In 1876, during Benjamin Disraeli's second term as prime minister of England, two of England's best novelists published books whose central characters were Jews. Neither George Eliot nor Anthony Trollope mentioned Disraeli by name in their Jewish novels. Yet for forty years, he had been by far the most prominent Jew in the country. In his books and speeches, Disraeli had tried to teach his countrymen his own peculiar way of thinking about Jews and Judaism. In his political career, he managed to turn his Jewishness, which his very name made it impossible to conceal, into a kind of asset. When Eliot and Trollope invented their Jewish protagonists, then, they were testifying, deliberately or not, to the imaginative climate that Disraeli had helped to create.

Daniel Deronda, the hero of George Eliot's great proto-Zionist novel, is by far the better known of the two characters. Daniel, when we first meet him, is a proud representative of a proud class, the English aristocracy. Yet he has always known that some mystery surrounds his birth. He was raised as the ward of Sir Hugo Mallinger, a rich and good-natured squire who is genuinely devoted to him; but while he suspects that he may be Sir Hugo's illegitimate son, he is never given any concrete information about his parentage. As he gets older, Eliot shows, the problem of his identity begins to prey on him more and more.

Daniel's thoughts are first turned to Judaism by his encounter with Mirah Lapidoth, a beautiful Jewish woman whom he rescues from a suicide attempt. Wanting to learn more about Mirah's people, he visits Frankfurt's old Jewish ghetto, the Judengasse, and wanders into the synagogue during a service. The spectacle of the praying congregation stirs violently contradictory emotions in Daniel. He is moved by the cantor's "grand wide-ranging voice with its passage from monotony to sudden cries," and seems to feel "a divine influx in the darkness." But at the same time, his English upbringing rebels against the "vulgar figures" of the Jews around him, the "queer-looking Israelites not altogether without guile" whom he has seen making deals and shouting in their "Jew-dialect." No wonder, then, that he is strangely affected when an old man in the synagogue lays a hand on his arm:

> he saw close to him the white-bearded face of that neighbour, who said to him in German, "Excuse me, young gentleman—allow me—what is your parentage—your mother's family—her maiden name?" Deronda had a strongly resistant feeling: he was inclined to shake off hastily the touch on his arm; but he managed to slip it away and said coldly, "I am an Englishman."

The idea that this German Jew might know him—might even know what he does not, the name of his mother—

appalls Daniel, and his response is meant to put the man in his place. To be an Englishman, and an English gentleman, is to belong to a different world than the Judengasse, and it is impossible that anyone should cross the boundary between them. Daniel feels the touch of the Jewish stranger as a violation, a claim of intimacy he is not willing to grant. He clutches at his Englishness like a talisman, or a life preserver.

But of course, in Eliot's novel as in a fairy tale, this stranger is really a messenger. For in time Daniel discovers that he, too, is a Jew. The old man, it turns out, had been a friend of his grandfather's, and his real mother is a famous Jewish actress, who gave her baby to Sir Hugo to raise. When Daniel finally meets his mother, in one of the novel's most powerful and frightening scenes, she explains that her reason for giving him up was to spare him the curse of being Jewish. "The bondage I hated for myself I wanted to keep you from," she says. "What better could the most loving mother have done? I relieved you from the bondage of being born a Jew." It is better to be a pretend Englishman, his mother insists, than a real Jew.

The lesson of *Daniel Deronda*, however, is that Jewishness is not "bondage"—or, at least, that it doesn't have to be. For the novel offers Daniel a different model of being Jewish than his mother's, with her self-hatred, or than the Frankfurt Jews', with their vulgar strangeness. This is the model of Mordecai, Mirah's brother, whose Judaism takes the form of a passionate Zionism. All the deficiencies of Jewish life, Mordecai believes, can be remedied by restoring the Jews to political existence: "Looking towards a land and a polity, our dispersed people in all the ends of the earth may share the dignity of a national life which has a voice among the peoples of the East and the West."

Years before Zionism became a political reality, it takes shape in Eliot's pages as a moral possibility. For in his dedication to restoring the Jewish homeland in Palestine, Mordecai purges himself of all the negative traits that Daniel and his creator associate with Jews. His example allows Daniel to claim the identity that his own mother urged him to hide. "It is no shame to have Jewish parents," he tells her, "the shame is to disown it." By the novel's end, Daniel has publicly declared his Jewishness and married Mirah, and he is about to set out for the East to work for Mordecai's dream. He may no longer be an English aristocrat, but now, thanks to the ennobling power of Zionism, he can be reborn as a kind of Jewish aristocrat: "It was as if he had found an added soul in finding his ancestry." Eliot insists that, contrary to popular belief, Jewishness and nobility are not mutually exclusive.

While George Eliot's readers were following the serial installments of *Daniel Deronda*, Anthony Trollope's audience thrilled to the machinations of a very different kind of Jew. Ferdinand Lopez, the villain of the fifth novel in Trollope's Palliser series, appears at first to be just as much of a gentleman as Daniel. Certainly he is presentable enough to win the heart of Emily Wharton, a young woman of pure English stock. As Trollope writes, ominously, "she sincerely believed that she had found the good man in Ferdinand Lopez. The man, certainly, was one strangely endowed with the power of creating a belief."

But Emily's father, the wealthy lawyer Mr. Wharton, recoils from the prospect of uniting his bloodline with that of Lopez. In fact, the most suspicious thing about Lopez is the way he never talks about his family or his origins. He admits to being half-Portuguese, but never to being what everyone can tell he is—a Jew. Like Desdemona's father in *Othello*, Mr. Wharton is filled with irrational disgust at the image of his daughter in a foreigner's arms. Yet he recognizes that this sort of instinctive revulsion is impossible to justify in the progressive nineteenth century. "It might be that it was a prejudice," he reasons. "Others probably did not find a man to be odious because he was of foreign extraction and known by a foreign name. Others would not suspect a man of being of Jewish blood because he was swarthy, or even object to him if he were a Jew by descent." And so, his foreboding held in check by his liberal scruples, Mr. Wharton allows Emily to marry Lopez.

Almost immediately, he discovers that his tolerance of a Jew has been a horrible mistake. Lopez turns out to be less like Daniel Deronda than like Marlowe's Jew of Malta. Greedy, vengeful, and dishonest, he is determined to squeeze his rich father-in-law for money to bail himself out of stock market speculations gone bad. As Mr. Wharton realizes the magnitude of his error, Trollope's descriptions of Lopez grow more and more hateful. He is "a man without a father, a foreigner, a black Portuguese nameless Jew," with "a bright eye, and a hook nose, and a glib tongue." His greed amounts to "thirsting for blood": "By God!" Mr. Wharton tells his daughter, "if there were money to be made by it I believe that he would murder you without scruple." And Lopez, like Shylock, fully returns this English and Christian hatred. "You know the Israelites despoiled the Egyptians, and it was taken as a merit on their part," he tells his wife. "Your father is an Egyptian to me, and I will despoil him."

But Trollope's most damning verdict on Ferdinand Lopez is not that he is a thieving, bloodthirsty Jew. It is that he is not a gentleman. If the moral of Eliot's novel is that a Jew can be a spiritual gentleman, the moral of Trollope's is that even a Jew who looks like a gentleman on the surface can never be one at heart. "In a sense [Lopez] was what is called a gentleman," he writes. "He knew how to speak, and how to look, how to use a knife and fork, how to dress himself, and how to walk. But he had not the faintest notion of the feelings of a gentleman." Instead of that honorable English title, Mr. Wharton realizes, Lopez deserves a different name: "And now it became clear to him that the man was . . . no better than an adventurer!"

The name of the novel in which Trollope created this adventurer, this Jew who prevails on the good nature of Englishmen only in order to trick and despoil them, is *The Prime Minister*. Ferdinand Lopez is not the title character; the prime minister in the novel is the Duke of Omnium, whose political career Trollope follows through the Palliser series.

But none of Trollope's readers, in 1876, would have found it hard to draw the connection between *The Prime Minister* and the Prime Minister, Benjamin Disraeli. The very questions that the novel poses—can a Jew be an Englishman? can Englishmen trust him?—had been asked about Disraeli since the beginning of his public life, almost fifty years earlier.

And the name Mr. Wharton hurls at Lopez—"adventurer"—was the very one that Disraeli's enemies constantly applied to him. In 1859, when Disraeli was Leader of the House of Commons, one of his opponents decried his parliamentary tactics: "There was a day when conduct of this kind would have been scouted as intolerable with unanimous scorn; but the House of Commons had never consented to be led by a Jew Adventurer." The Marquess of Salisbury, a Conservative who succeeded Disraeli as prime minister, echoed that judgment: "he is an adventurer: & as I have too good cause to know, he is without principles and honesty." Disraeli was under no illusions about what his colleagues thought of him. "I am Disraeli the adventurer," he ruefully said during a party intrigue, "and I will not acquiesce in a position which will enable the party to make use of me in debate, and then throw me aside."

In fact, Disraeli himself makes an appearance in Trollope's novel, thinly disguised as Mr. Daubeny, the leader of the Conservatives in the House of Commons. (The Parliamentary combat between Mr. Daubeny and Mr. Gresham, as Trollope calls Disraeli's great rival, William Ewart Gladstone, is a running feature of the Palliser novels.) While

Daubeny is not explicitly Jewish, Trollope describes him in the same equivocal terms that were always applied to his original. "I have always felt that there has been a mistake about Mr. Daubeny," says one of the novel's many scheming politicians. "By many he has been accounted as a statesman, whereas to me he has always been a political Cagliostro"—an English equivalent of the eighteenth-century Italian con man and self-proclaimed magician. "Now a conjuror is I think a very pleasant fellow to have among us, if we know that he is a conjuror—but a conjuror who is believed to do his tricks without sleight of hand is a dangerous man."

Conjuror, like adventurer, was another popular term of abuse for Disraeli; to Thomas Carlyle, he was "a superlative Hebrew conjuror." Indeed, Disraeli overcame so many obstacles on his path to power that his triumph seemed like something that should not have been able to happen, something only magic could explain. He was not actually born into the lowest ranks of English society; his grandfather was a wealthy businessman, and his father was a well-connected man of letters. But no Prime Minister in the nineteenth century had a longer or more difficult route to power.

Many of the obstacles Disraeli faced along the way, however, were self-created. He first became famous, at the age of just twenty-one, as the author of a scandalous novel, *Vivian Grey*, whose indiscreet confession of his boundless ambition haunted him for the rest of his life. As a young man, he contracted enormous debts that he couldn't hope to repay, and only narrowly avoided prison. He carried on love affairs with married women, and according to rumor, even traded one of his mistresses to a leading Tory in exchange for political favors. A follower of the cult of Byron, he was willfully extravagant in dress and conversation. All of these things helped to mark Disraeli out as unconventional, unpredictable, and therefore untrustworthy. That such a man rose to become prime minister, during the famously earnest Victorian age, did seem like a magician's feat. Even so, it took him a very long time. He was in Parliament for thirty years before his first brief stint as prime minister, and he was nearly seventy years old before he was elected to a full term of office.

But the words that Disraeli's opponents used to attack him also suggest the strange respect that he inspired. After all, what is an adventurer but a man who rises in the world despite the odds? What is a conjuror but a man so brilliant that ordinary minds can't understand how he does what he does? Gladstone captured this ambiguity when he spoke, half-admiringly, of Disraeli's "diabolical cleverness." To a sympathetic eye, Disraeli's success in politics might look like a testament to English meritocracy, which allowed even a Jew to rise to the heights of power. In 1868, when he became prime minister for the first time, Queen Victoria congratulated him in just those terms: "It must be a proud moment for him to feel that his own talent and successful labours in the service of his Sovereign and country have earned for him the high and influential position in which he is now placed." Or, as the French statesman Guizot told him: "I think your being the leader of the Tory party is the greatest triumph that Liberalism has ever achieved."

Yet Disraeli, who lived during the glory days of English Liberalism, was a dedicated foe of liberal ideas. He did not believe in what he called "the equivocal principle of religious liberty," and he zealously defended the established Church of England. His political allies were the landowners he admiringly called "the gentlemen of England," and he fought against every encroachment on their privileges. He made his political reputation opposing free trade, and spent decades opposing universal suffrage. While the Liberals applauded the struggles for independence in Italy and Poland, Disraeli remained hostile, chalking up the continent-wide movement toward national liberation to the schemes of "secret societies." In his novels, he even dreamed of a feudal restoration in England—a future in which the power of Parliament would be curtailed and the power of the monarch restored, while a contented peasantry deferred to its natural leaders.

If a politician's success is measured solely by his ability to translate his ideals into reality, then Disraeli the politician would have to be judged a failure. As a critic of Victorian utilitarianism and materialism, Disraeli ranks with the prophet-sages of his era—Carlyle, Arnold, Ruskin, and the other great writers who pointed out the spiritual and social costs of England's progress. Yet his idealism was no more capable than theirs of halting the momentum of the age. Gladstone, who began his career as a Tory and ended up as a radical Liberal, was right when he harangued Disraeli and the Conservatives: "You cannot fight against the future. Time is on our side. The great social forces which move onward in their might and majesty and which the tumult of your debates does not for a moment impede or disturb . . . are against you."

The difference, of course, is that Disraeli was not just a critic of the Victorian age but one of its leading politicians. As a leader of the Conservative Party, he had to balance ideals against possibilities; and as a very ambitious man, he was usually ready to make compromises to achieve power. His greatest legislative achievement was the passage of the Second Reform Bill in 1867, which gave the right to vote to most male heads of households—a measure more liberal than even the Liberals had been ready to contemplate. It was the accomplishment that made Disraeli prime minister, but to diehard Conservatives like Salisbury, it was also "a political betrayal that has no parallel in our Parliamentary annals." The result was that Disraeli laid himself open to charges of opportunism and hypocrisy, compounding the distrust he already inspired—as a novelist, a dandy, an adventurer, and, of course, a Jew.

For Disraeli's Jewishness was the central fact about him, the thing that no one could ever forget or ignore. "No Englishman," one of his contemporaries wrote, "could approach Disraeli without some immediate consciousness that he was in the presence of a foreigner." It didn't matter that he was born in London, like his father before him, or that he spoke no language but English. It didn't even matter that he was, in fact, a practicing Christian, baptized at the age of twelve into the Church of England. As a Jew, Disraeli belonged to a foreign race, distinguished by his appearance—and, many believed, by his values and ways of thinking—from the nation he led. "He never became wholly assimilated to English ways of life," wrote Winston Churchill, as though he remained a permanent immigrant in the country of his birth.

The way Disraeli's physical difference seemed to mark a spiritual difference is perfectly captured by the description that one observer, Sir John Skelton, left of Disraeli's visit to Scotland in 1867: "And the potent wizard himself, with his olive complexion and coal-black eyes, and the mighty dome of his forehead (no Christian temple, be sure), is unlike any living creature one has met. . . . The face is more like a mask than ever, and the division between him and mere mortals more marked. I would as soon have thought of sitting down at table with Hamlet, or Lear, or the Wandering Jew."

Yet significantly, Skelton went on to rebuke those who considered Disraeli "an alien" and asked, "What's England to him, or he to England?" Disraeli did, in fact, have England's interests at heart, Skelton insisted: "England is the Israel of his imagination." The phrase seems to sum up all the ambiguities of Disraeli's life and career, and also to suggest the way he mastered them. Knowing that his Jewishness was indelible—that it was written in his name and on his face—he never attempted to hide it. To try to do so, he

Disraeli as prime minister, 1875:
The potent wizard himself.
*Courtesy of the Print Collection, Miriam and
Ira D. Wallach Division of Art, Prints, and Photographs,
The New York Public Library, Astor, Lenox
and Tilden Foundations.*

knew, would not only be futile; in the eyes of the English gentlemen who were his peers, it would seem disgraceful. Ferdinand Lopez's first sin, after all, was to conceal his parentage. A man who could do that was capable of anything. Instead, Disraeli chose Daniel Deronda's path, insisting that it was no shame to be Jewish, only to disown it.

But unlike Eliot's hero, Disraeli did not want to escape his English milieu and become a strictly Jewish leader. (He even made a point of telling people he had not read Eliot's book: "When I want to read a novel, I write one," he joked.) The dream of what was not yet called Zionism had a powerful allure for Disraeli, and two of his novels, *Alroy* and *Tancred*, belong with *Daniel Deronda* in the proto-Zionist canon. But while he fantasized about restoring the Jews to a political existence in Palestine, neither the conditions of Jewish life in Europe nor his own personality allowed Disraeli to play the role that would eventually fall to Theodor Herzl. England offered what Palestine could not: a theater for immediate action, where power could actually be won.

To achieve that goal, however, Disraeli would need more than mere tolerance from his countrymen. Such cold respect might satisfy the leading English Jews of his day—rich worthies like the Rothschilds and Montefiores, who steadily asserted their right to legal equality and finally won it. Disraeli, whose ambition gave him no rest even as a teenager, did not want to be treated as an equal. He wanted to be admired as a superior, to lead men and control the destiny of empires. And that meant that he had to turn his Jewishness from a handicap into a mystique. He had to convince the world, and himself, that the Jews were a noble race, with a glorious past and a great future. He even had to turn anti-Semitic myths to his own account—to make people believe that, if he was a wizard and a conjuror, he would at least use his powers for England. As a result, Disraeli became one of the nineteenth century's chief points of reference for thinking about Jews and Judaism. Jews and anti-Semites alike looked to Disraeli in constructing their own images of Jewish power.

Disraeli's life story has been told many times—first of all by himself, in his veiled autobiographical novels, and then by a long series of biographers and historians. Usually, it is told as an English story, for obvious reasons. He made his mark on history as a British statesman, and his political accomplishments are, as it were, the content of his achievement. But to appreciate the significance of his achievement, it is necessary to understand Disraeli's life as a Jewish story.

For Disraeli's Jewishness was both the greatest obstacle to his ambition and its greatest engine. It inspired his most original ideas about politics and history, while insuring that his very originality made him a perpetual outsider in the country he rose to lead. He was, as Hannah Arendt wrote, the preeminent example of the nineteenth-century phenomenon of "exception Jews"—assimilated Jews who imposed themselves on Europe through the force of their genius, but were never allowed to move beyond imposition to genuine, unexceptional belonging. In this sense, Disraeli's career was a perfect emblem of both the possibilities of emancipation for European Jewry, and its subtle impossibilities.

In this book, then, while I trace the contour of his career and examine some of its chief episodes, I devote more attention to Disraeli the Jewish writer and thinker than to Disraeli the practical politician. Now that the issues that occupied his professional life have receded into history, it is Disraeli's imagination of power that makes him an enduringly provocative figure. In telling his story, I hope to show why the tribute paid to Disraeli by one of his rivals still holds true: "To the imagination of the younger generation your life will always have a special fascination. For them you have enlarged the horizon of the possibilities of the future."

Benjamin Disraeli

1

The man who preceded Benjamin Disraeli as leader of Britain's Conservative Party was Edward Stanley, the 14th Earl of Derby. His family had held that title since 1485, when Thomas Stanley earned it by switching sides during the Battle of Bosworth Field, helping Henry VII to defeat Richard III. In Shakespeare's play, it is Stanley's refusal to come to Richard's aid that dooms him—"What says Lord Stanley? will he bring his power?" Richard begs, just before crying "my kingdom for a horse"—and it is Stanley who places the crown on the head of the first Tudor monarch: "Lo, here, this long-usurped royalty / From the dead temples of this bloody wretch / Have I pluck'd off, to grace thy brows withal. / Wear it, enjoy it, and make much of it."

For men like Derby, who continued to govern the country throughout the nineteenth century, Shakespeare was not just England's national poet. He was the chronicler of their own families, writing about events in which their ancestors had taken leading parts. For Disraeli, of course, encountering Shakespeare was a very different experience. As a young boy, he attended a school run by an Independent minister—a broad-minded place, where he and another Jewish student were excused from Christian prayers and received weekly

Hebrew lessons from a rabbi. Yet even this tolerant school-master saw no objection to assigning young Ben the part of Gratiano in a school production of *The Merchant of Venice.* Evidently Disraeli did not give a good performance, perhaps on account of some the speeches he had to deliver. In the trial scene, for instance, Gratiano berates Shylock:

> O, be thou damn'd, inexecrable dog!
> And for thy life let justice be accused.
> Thou almost makest me waver in my faith
> To hold opinion with Pythagoras,
> That souls of animals infuse themselves
> Into the trunks of men: thy currish spirit
> Govern'd a wolf, who, hang'd for human slaughter,
> Even from the gallows did his fell soul fleet,
> And, whilst thou lay'st in thy unhallow'd dam,
> Infused itself in thee; for thy desires
> Are wolvish, bloody, starved and ravenous.

What effect did it have on Disraeli to recite these lines, the closest thing England's national poet offered to a description of his ancestors? It is impossible to say for sure; as a grown man, he almost never wrote directly about his childhood. But in *Tancred*, the novel in which he deals most extensively with Jewish subjects, his Jewish heroine Eva makes an unusually heartfelt speech about childhood. "They say that the children of our race are the most beautiful in the world, but that when they grow up, they do not fulfill the promise of their infancy," she says. "It is the sense of shame that comes on them and dims their lustre. Instead of joyousness and frank hilarity, anxiety and a shrinking reserve are soon impressed upon the youthful Hebrew visage. . . . The dreadful secret that they are an expatriated and persecuted race is soon revealed to them, at least among the humbler classes."

But Eva goes on to insist that "the children of our house are bred in noble thoughts, and taught self-respect. Their countenances will not change." And Disraeli, from the moment he emerged as a public figure at the age of twenty-one, was remarkable for his self-respect, which did not falter under the most ferocious personal and political attacks. One source of that strength was his certainty of his own gifts. Equally important, however, was the way Disraeli imagined Jews and Jewishness, countering the myth of Jewish vulgarity and greed with an empowering myth of Jewish talent and influence.

The English were a receptive audience for such myths, because the English imagination of Jews had long been divorced from any actual knowledge of them. In 1290, King Edward I expelled the Jews from England, driving out a community that had long been subject to both popular persecution and royal confiscations. For the next three and a half centuries, there were no Jews in England, with the exception of the occasional traveler or merchant. As a result, the images of Jews in classic English literature—from Chaucer's Prioress's Tale, with its gruesome account of ritual murder, to Marlowe's mass-murdering Jew of Malta, to Shakespeare's merciless Shylock—were created in a vacuum, built of nothing but fantasy and inherited prejudice.

The same ignorance of actual Jews informed the eccentric but persistent strain of English philo-Semitism, which led some Puritan divines to believe that the readmission of the Jews to England would help to usher in the messianic age. This sentiment helped to influence Oliver Cromwell's decision, in 1656, to allow the Jews to return to England. In typically pragmatic English fashion, Cromwell never issued an official edict defining the status of Jews; instead, he informally encouraged the efforts of Menasseh ben Israel, a Sephardic Jew from Amsterdam, to reestablish a Jewish community in London. Because the laws of England never officially took cognizance of the Jews, then, there was no legal discrimination for them to overcome. As a result, by the beginning of the nineteenth century, Jews in England uncontroversially enjoyed almost all the rights that Jews on the Continent had only recently and precariously won: they could own land, testify in court, and practice most trades. Only a few privileges remained out of their reach—above all, the right to sit in Parliament, which still required an oath "upon the true faith of a Christian."

The main reason why the "Jewish question" didn't arise in England, however, was that England had a smaller Jewish population than any other major European country. The initial wave of Sephardic immigrants, from Spain and Portugal by way of Holland, was followed in the eighteenth century by a steady stream of Ashkenazi Jews from Germany and

Poland. Yet by the early nineteenth century, there were still only some fifteen thousand Jews in Britain, out of a total population of twelve million. (At the same period, there were about forty thousand Jews in France, and two hundred thousand in Germany.) Most English people—especially outside London, where some two-thirds of English Jews lived—could easily spend their whole lives without ever coming into contact with a Jew.

Overt religious prejudice had waned since the days of Cromwell, when opponents of Jewish readmission warned that the Jews were planning to purchase St. Paul's Cathedral and turn it into a synagogue. But the dominant Jewish stereotypes of Disraeli's day, while less venomous, were scarcely more flattering. On the one hand, there were a few extremely rich English Jewish families—Rothschilds, Salomons, and Goldsmids, whose role in international finance inspired fantasy and suspicion. On the other, there was the vast majority of poor Jews, who scraped by selling cheap goods and secondhand clothes. A pamphlet published in 1795 gives a sense of the widespread English contempt for such Jewish peddlers: "we see them wandering about the streets, particularly in the metropolis of London, in the most menial occupation, that of carrying a bag at their back, and crying old cloaths from door to door, the objects of universal ridicule and contempt . . . even children despise them and laugh them to scorn."

For Disraeli, whose pride was his ruling passion, it was imperative to escape the only models of Jewishness that

English culture offered him—the "wolvish, bloody" image of Shylock and the ridiculous, contemptible image of the old-clothes man. Instead, he determined to invent his own image of Jewishness, by endowing the Disraelis with the antiquity and stature of the Stanleys. As a Sephardic Jew, he asserted, his family line was even older than those of the Norman barons who came to England in 1066. It could be dated to the ancient world: "The tradition . . . that the Iberian Jews were a Phoenician colony has been favoured by the researches of modern antiquaries," he wrote. What's more, the Jews of Spain were not mere merchants, but landowners, just like the great families of England: "It appears by a decree of Constantine that they were owners and cultivators of the soil, a circumstance which alone proves the antiquity and the nobility of their settlement, for the possession of the land is never conceded to a degraded race."

The Disraeli family, Benjamin wrote in a memoir of his father, belonged to this ancient race of squires. Forced to leave Spain when the Jews were expelled in 1492, they found asylum in Venice. That was when "his ancestors had dropped their Gothic surname on their settlement in the Terra Firma, and grateful to the God of Jacob who had sustained them through unprecedented trials and guarded them through unheard-of perils, they assumed the name of DISRAELI, a name never borne before, or since, by any other family, in order that their race might be for ever recognised."

This was a founding myth of which even an English nobleman could be proud. The scene of that ancestor crowning himself with the name Disraeli was a Jewish version of Thomas Stanley crowning Henry VII, or even Napoléon taking the imperial diadem from the pope's hands and placing it on his own head. Disraeli used it to justify adopting a heraldic coat of arms: he once wrote that "The tower (Castle) of *Castille*, which I use as a crest, and which was taken from one of the quarters of my shield, was adopted" by one of his ancestors in the sixteenth century.

It made no difference, for Disraeli's purposes, that this family history was completely invented. In fact, as later researchers have discovered, there is no evidence that the Disraelis came from Spain, and they did not live in Venice. As far back as it can be traced, the family lived in the town of Cento, in the Papal States. Nor were they actually named Disraeli. It was Benjamin's grandfather who adopted the more distinguished-sounding "D'Israeli" when he moved to England. Before that, they were simply Israeli, a name commonly bestowed on Jews in Arabic-speaking lands. Most likely, they came from the Middle East.

Yet if the Castilian castle on Disraeli's crest was illegitimate, the Latin motto he chose to accompany it was entirely appropriate: *Forti nihil difficile*, nothing is difficult to the brave. Disraeli's readiness to invent a genealogy for himself was a perfect example of his refusal to be daunted. He recognized that pride of family was one of the sources of strength that enabled the English ruling class to govern so confidently, even in an increasingly democratic age. "When a man raises his eyes from his bench and sees his ancestor in the tapestry," he wrote in an early novel, "he begins to understand the pride of blood."

Nor would he have considered it exactly dishonest to embellish his ancestry, when so many Englishmen did the same thing. Few noble pedigrees, in the Victorian period, could be traced back as far as the Tudors, and many a nineteenth-century lord bought his peerage after making a fortune in railroads or banking. Such titles threw a "halo of imagination," as Disraeli put it, over "many a humble or obscure origin." A running joke in his novel *Sybil* is that young Lord Fitz-Warene—"the most aristocratic of breathing beings," who "most fully, entirely, and absolutely believed in his pedigree"—is actually the son of a former waiter, John Warren, who went out to India as a gentleman's valet and defrauded the natives out of so much money that he could afford to buy a title.

Disraeli could make fun of the convenient amnesia that allowed English society to consider any rich man a gentleman. But he also recognized that this class mobility was what allowed the English aristocracy, unlike its Continental equivalents, to function as a kind of meritocracy. "It is not true that England is governed by an aristocracy in the common acceptation of the term," he insisted. "England is governed by an aristocratic principle. The aristocracy of England absorbs all aristocracies, and receives every man in every order and every class who defers to the principle of our society, which is to aspire and to excel."

Disraeli's own family offered a perfect example of that principle in action. His grandfather Benjamin D'Israeli came to England in 1748 at the age of eighteen. He married twice, each time into a wealthy Sephardic family, and the resulting dowries and connections enabled him to make a small fortune as a stockbroker. His grandson imagined that, with a little more persistence, he might have turned it into a big fortune—that the Disraelis might have ended up like the Rothschilds, who took advantage of the opportunities provided by the Napoleonic Wars to build a financial empire. "That, however, was not our destiny," Disraeli wrote wistfully. Still, Benjamin D'Israeli left behind enough money to ensure that neither his son nor his grandson ever had to work for a living.

For Isaac D'Israeli, son and father of Benjamins, that leisure was precious because it allowed him to devote his life to literature. Isaac spent so much of his time reading and writing that he seems, in his son's account, almost ethereal. Yet he turned his obsessive bookworming to good account, even becoming a minor celebrity when, at the age of twenty-five, he published his best-selling *Curiosities of Literature.* To produce this anthology of literary anecdotes and historical trivia, Isaac combed through the library of the British Museum for interesting tidbits, then turned them into miniature essays on subjects ranging from "Literary Forgeries" to "On the Custom of Kissing Hands." The book went through twelve steadily expanding editions, and Isaac extended the franchise with *Calamities of Authors, Quarrels of Authors,* and other spin-offs. These works gave him a respected place in the literary world, and won him the admiration of Lord Byron, among others. "I don't know a living man's book I take up so often, or lay down more reluctantly, as Israeli's," Byron told their common publisher, John Murray.

Byron's way of spelling Isaac's name, however, pointed to the continuing anomaly of his presence as a Jew in English literary culture. Byron did not necessarily mean to emphasize the word "Israel" at the heart of Isaac D'Israeli's name, or to slight the noble-sounding particle. But Isaac's son was highly sensitive to such nuances. In 1832, when Benjamin Disraeli's fame was beginning to rival his father's, a magazine called *The Omnibus* published an alphabetical catalogue of prominent writers. In a letter to his older sister, Sarah, Benjamin quoted the entry for "I": "I is Israeli, a man of great gumption,/To leave out the D is a piece of assumption."

Already, it seems, people knew that Benjamin Disraeli did not like to be known as simply Israeli. Indeed, it was Benjamin who changed the spelling of the family name from D'Israeli to Disraeli, when he was eighteen years old. The new spelling did not, of course, conceal the Jewishness of the name, but by bringing the capital I down to lowercase, and running the particle D' into the name itself, the change does look like a symbolic attempt to reduce the centrality of the word "Israel." This would seem far-fetched, perhaps, if it were not for Disraeli's response when *Fraser's Magazine* published an article about Isaac that referred to him as

"Israel D'Israeli"—"which leads to an observation or two," he commented to his sister. Such a mistake effectively squared the Jewishness of the name, just as Benjamin was trying to minimize it. Indeed, if the error was inadvertent, it was all the more revealing, suggesting how thoroughly Englishmen associated the D'Israeli family with the name and people of Israel.

Even the way Benjamin spelled it, however, the name Disraeli was like a placard announcing his foreignness. This remained true even when he had become one of the most famous men in England. In 1867, at the height of the debate over the Second Reform Bill, his secretary wrote him a letter from the provinces: "Your name is in the mouth of every labourer, who, without knowing what 'Reform' means, or caring, hears that Mr. ———— has won a great victory. I leave the blank, as it is impossible to express the Protean variety which a name, revered and cherished by me, here assumes." The people Disraeli governed could not pronounce his name. It was partly for this reason, and partly as a tribute to his unsettling brilliance, that he was widely known by his nickname—Dizzy.

2

In addition to a Jewish name, Isaac D'Israeli bequeathed his son a painfully ambivalent attitude toward Judaism. As Disraeli put it later in life, "I was not bred among my race, and was nurtured in great prejudice against them." Isaac, born in 1766, belonged to the first generation of emancipated Jews. He was an admirer of Moses Mendelssohn, the German-Jewish prophet of Enlightenment, and drank deep of the anticlerical rationalism of Voltaire. These influences, which helped to draw him away from traditional Jewish observance, met with no countervailing pull in his childhood home. In general, the Jews of England were one of the least observant communities in Europe: thanks to their small numbers, their distance from major Jewish centers, and the comparative ease of assimilation, the standard of piety and learning among English Jews was notoriously low. In the late eighteenth century, the rabbi of the main Ashkenazi synagogue in London complained that there wasn't a single person in the country with whom he could discuss the Talmud.

Disraeli himself was a prime example of this unfamiliarity with Jewish traditions. Yet with typical ingenuity, he would manage to turn his ignorance into a source of freedom. The eccentric understanding of Jewishness that Disraeli bequeathed the world was in large part his own invention, and the way he writes about Jews in his novels is frequently fantastic. His imagination of Jewish history, including his inklings of what would become political Zionism, could not have been so daring if he had been tethered more closely to actualities.

Certainly Disraeli did not inherit any family tradition of Jewish observance. Isaac's father, Disraeli wrote, "appears never to have cordially or intimately mixed with his community." And Isaac's mother, Sarah, was actively hostile to Judaism, as Disraeli explained: "My grandmother, the beautiful daughter of a family who had suffered from persecution, had imbibed that dislike for her race which the vain are too apt to adopt when they find that they are born to public contempt." Marriage to a man named D'Israeli only made things worse, and she "never pardoned" her husband for his name. Sarah's bitterness made her an unpleasant and disliked figure in the family, "so mortified by her social position that she lived until eighty without indulging in a tender expression." The young Ben hated going to her house, where there was "no kindness, no tea, no tips—nothing." It was a powerful lesson about the price of Jewish self-hatred, which he was never to forget.

What about Disraeli's own mother, Maria? We don't know about her attitude toward Judaism, or whether she performed any of the rituals traditionally assigned to the mother in a Jewish household. In fact, we know almost nothing about Disraeli's mother, for the simple reason that he never mentioned her. Maria Basevi, whom Isaac married in 1802, came from a more distinguished family than her husband's. Indeed, the Basevis actually had the ancient Spanish connections that Benjamin invented for the Disraelis. Maria was descended, through her mother, from Isaac Aboab, the last gaon of Castile, who helped to negotiate passage to Portugal for thousands of Spanish Jews expelled by Ferdinand and Isabella. The Basevis were also related by marriage to many of the families that dominated Anglo-Jewish high society, such as the Montefiores.

If Disraeli played down this side of his family history, it may be because he seemed determined to erase his mother from his biography. He often talked about his father, whom he genuinely admired and loved, but he had nothing to say, good or bad, about his mother. He didn't mention her even once in his extended essay on his father's life, written as a preface to a posthumous edition of Isaac's works. His sister Sarah protested at the omission: "I do wish that one felicitous stroke, one tender word had brought our dear Mother into the picture."

What resentments lay behind this pointed silence? It is impossible to say for sure, but Disraeli's fiction contains several portraits of unappreciative, unaffectionate mothers. "Mark what blunders parents constantly make as to the nature of their own offspring, bred, too, under their own eyes, and displaying every hour their characteristics," Disraeli complains in his novel *Coningsby*. "How often in the nursery does the genius count as a dunce because he is pensive; while a rattling urchin is invested with almost supernatural qualities because his animal spirits make him impudent and flippant!" Does this passage echo Disraeli's own sense that his mother did not, could not, recognize his extraordinary gifts? It is certain, at least, that throughout his adult life Disraeli looked for replacement mother figures. His closest relationships, including love affairs, were with older women who babied and doted on him.

It was Isaac, then, whose complex feelings about Judaism did most to shape his son's. His ambivalence, which he shared with Jews of his generation all over Western Europe, is the constant subtext of Isaac's only book on a Jewish subject—*The Genius of Judaism*, published in 1833. It is invaluable as a document of the contradictory messages that the young Disraeli must have absorbed from his father. On the one hand, as the title suggests, *The Genius of Judaism* was written as a vindication of Isaac's religion, and an attempt to educate Englishmen about the mysterious subjects of Jewish history and theology. "The genius of Judaism," he writes, "has remained veiled to the Christian, as if the shekinah still was resting in 'the holy of holies.' "

Yet the book is also, essentially, a brief for assimilation. "The Hebrew separated from the Christian, at a period of the highest civilisation, holds an anomalous position in society," Isaac writes on the first page, and the pain of that anomaly is reflected in his sarcastic treatment of traditional Jewish learning and customs. He can find something to admire in biblical Judaism, which was the national creed of a sovereign state. He even suggests that the Israelite common-wealth was a model government: "During the theocracy, this agrestic and military people preserved that political equality which human institutions have vainly attempted to realise under the forms of popular government." In its proto-Zionism, and its suggestion that submission to a divine order is the only true freedom, this theory of Isaac's was to prove deeply influential on his son's political thought.

But after the Roman conquest, Isaac believes, the basis for a dignified national existence disappeared, and Judaism entered its dark ages. "Built up with all the strength and the subtility, but with all the abuse of the human understanding; founded on the infirmities of our nature, a system of superstitions has immersed the Hebrews in a mass of ritual ordinances, casuistical glosses, and arbitrary decisions, hardly equalled by their subsequent mimics of the papistry." Isaac's association of rabbinical Judaism with "casuistical" Catholicism is an ingenious rhetorical stroke, allowing him to appeal to both the Voltairean spirit of anti-clericalism and the traditional English Protestant suspicion of the pope. To hate the Talmud in this spirit is not to hate Judaism, Isaac suggests, but to hate obscurantism. In another work, he refers to the Talmud as "a complete system of the barbarous learning of the Jews."

The question is how Jews in the modern world are to deal with this barbarous legacy. Isaac's answer is straightforward: they must "amalgamate" with modern European society. There is no reason, he assures his readers, why Jews cannot become good Englishmen: "After a few generations the Hebrews assimilate with the character, and are actuated by the feelings, of the nation where they become natives." But in exchange for this opportunity to assimilate, Isaac demands that the Jews disembarrass themselves of their obsolete traditions. "I would implore the Jews," he writes, "to begin to educate their youth as the youth of Europe, and not of Palestine; let their Talmud be removed to an elevated shelf, to be consulted as a curiosity of antiquity, and not as a manual of education."

Perhaps the most eloquent part of that plea is the pronouns: "their" and not "our," Isaac writes, as though he were not himself one of "the Jews." He is still more evasive when he writes, "Let those who are born in the happy faith of Christianity compassionate the Jew, for we cannot relieve him." Elsewhere in *The Genius of Judaism*, however, his grammar is tellingly ambiguous. "In Judaism we trace our Christianity, and in Christianity we are reminded of our Judaism," Isaac writes, as though he were both Christian and Jew. This insistence that Christianity and Judaism are inextricable, that the Christian cannot be fully Christian without acknowledging his Jewish roots, would become another important part of Benjamin Disraeli's thinking about Judaism. In 1847, arguing for the right of Jews to sit in Parliament, Disraeli echoed his father: "Who are these persons professing the Jewish religion? They are persons who acknowledge the same God as the Christian people of this realm. They acknowledge the same divine revelation as yourselves. They are, humanly speaking, the authors of your religion."

It might seem that, given Isaac's freethinking and his views on "amalgamation," there was nothing stopping him from simply converting to Christianity. Yet oddly, throughout *The Genius of Judaism*, he writes with unmistakable scorn about converts. He notes with satisfaction that the Society for Promoting Christianity Among the Jews "had not procured more than *six proselytes annually.*" Although he regrets the Jews' determination to be "a peculiar people"—which he calls "the real cause of the universal hatred which the Hebrews have excited in every nation and every age"—he is also, illogically, proud of it. "A single step only divides Judaism from Christianity," he writes, "but Heaven has interposed, and for 'the son of the covenant,' that step no human effort shall pass."

It is hard to imagine what Isaac must have been feeling when he wrote those words, knowing that all four of his children had taken that "single step," because he made them take it. Benjamin, his first son, was born on December 21, 1804, and was circumcised according to Jewish law. But in 1817, the summer before he would have been Bar Mitzvah, Isaac had Benjamin baptized in the Church of England— along with his older sister, Sarah, and his two younger brothers, Ralph and James. Thus Benjamin Disraeli, the most famous of English Jews, was actually a Christian for his entire adult life. Indeed, if he hadn't been, he would never have become famous, at least not as a politician: when Disraeli launched his political career, Jews were legally barred from sitting in Parliament.

Isaac's decision to have his children baptized, then, could not have been more momentous. But the reason behind it was oddly trivial. Isaac, like all Sephardic Jews in London, belonged to the Bevis Marks Synagogue, the oldest Jewish congregation in England. In 1813, he was chosen to serve as *parnas*, or warden, of the synagogue; if he declined the office, he was supposed to pay a fine. But Isaac refused to do either, choosing instead to denounce the synagogue in an angry letter. He was, he wrote, "a person . . . who can never unite in your public worship, because, as now conducted, it disturbs, instead of exciting, religious emotions, a circumstance of general acknowledgment; who has only tolerated some part of your ritual, willing to concede all he can in those matters which he holds to be indifferent." But "such a man," he went on, "never can accept the solemn functions of an Elder in your congregation, and involve his life . . . in permanent duties always repulsive to his feelings."

In this letter, we can see all the ambivalence that would later emerge in *The Genius of Judaism*. It is as though Isaac were warning the synagogue that he would consent to be a Jew only if he could be one passively; press him to act, and he might well decide to quit the congregation entirely. Four years later, in 1817, when the synagogue again tried to compel him to pay a fine, that is just what he did. Once Isaac was out of Bevis Marks, he seemed content to simply remain a nonobservant Jew. But a friend persuaded him that he owed his children, at least, the opportunities that only baptism could provide. For them, if not for himself, he decided to claim what Heinrich Heine called "a ticket of admission to European culture."

How did Disraeli feel about this life-changing step? Some biographers, noting that his baptism took place a few weeks after his younger brothers', speculate that he may have fought Isaac's decision; and it does seem likely that the ritual, which would have meant nothing to the four-year-old James, might have troubled the precocious twelve-year-old Ben. But there is no way of finding out just what caused the delay, or whether it had any cause at all. What is certain is that, in his fiction, Disraeli writes about converts and conversion even more contemptuously than his father did. In his novel *Alroy*, Disraeli shows the hero resisting an unscrupulous friend's advice to convert to Islam for the sake of power: "Is this thy high contempt of our poor kind, to outrage my God! to prove myself the vilest of the vile, and baser than the basest?"

Did Disraeli pass the same kind of judgment on himself? Reading this and other passages in his fiction, it is hard to avoid suspecting that at moments he did. But self-contempt was alien to his nature, and he had two powerful justifications for refusing it. The first was that, as a twelve-year-old, he could not really be held responsible for the decision to be baptized. It was his father, not himself, who incurred the odium of conversion. This may even have been Isaac's real motivation for quitting the synagogue in such a seemingly capricious way: it allowed him to have Ben baptized on the threshold of adulthood, before the decision could be laid psychologically and morally to his son's account. Isaac may have felt just as Theodor Herzl did when Herzl wrote in his diary almost a century later: "I myself would never convert, yet I am in favor of conversion. . . . One must baptize Jewish boys before they must account for themselves, before they are able to act against it and before conversion can be construed as weakness on their part."

The second way that Disraeli dealt with whatever shame he may have felt about escaping from Judaism was more ingenious and more significant. Knowing that he could never "pass" as an ordinary Christian, Disraeli evolved a complex public image that allowed him to remain a Jew, even while enjoying the legal rights of a member of the Church of England. As he put it in one of his most celebrated witticisms, "I am the blank page between the Old Testament and the New." The image was not his own—it came from a play by Richard Brinsley Sheridan—-but it perfectly captured Disraeli's ambiguous place in English society. Like that page, he could serve as a bridge between Judaism and Christianity only because he didn't quite belong to either; and he dealt with their irreconcilable claims by maintaining the elusiveness of a blank.

But not its muteness. On the contrary, Disraeli wrote and spoke extensively, especially in the first half of his career, about his idiosyncratic religious views. His central point was always that Judaism and Christianity are essentially one faith, and he insisted that each religion should acknowledge its dependence on the other. As an Anglican priest argues in *Sybil*, "the second Testament is avowedly only a supplement. Jehovah-Jesus came to complete the 'law and the prophets.' Christianity is completed Judaism, or it is nothing. Christianity is incomprehensible without Judaism, as Judaism is incomplete without Christianity." This theologically dubious argument won no adherents among either believing Christians or believing Jews. But it was psychologically necessary for Disraeli to make it, if he was to pull off the delicate balancing act required of a Jew seeking to lead a Christian nation.

Officially, Disraeli was a member in good standing of the Church of England. He attended church on Sundays, though not as eagerly as his rival, Gladstone, and he took Communion. This adherence is what allowed him to take the oath required of every member of the House of Commons until 1858, which contained the words "upon the true faith of a Christian." When he spoke of "our religion" or "our church," he always meant Protestantism and the Church of England. "Upon our acceptance of that Divine interpretation for which we are indebted to the Church, and of which the Church is the guardian," he said in one of his most famous speeches, "all sound and salutary legislation depends."

But Disraeli's Christianity did not stop him from acknowledging—indeed, insisting—that he was a Jew. He squared this circle by reimagining Jewishness as a matter of race rather than belief. When he spoke of "my race," as opposed to "our religion," he meant the Jews, not the English. He would have agreed with Moses Hess, who wrote, in his pioneering Zionist essay *Rome and Jerusalem*, that "Judaism as a nationality has a natural basis which cannot be set aside by mere conversion to another faith, as is the case in other religions. A Jew belongs to his race and consequently also to Judaism, in spite of the fact that he or his ancestors have become apostates." This principle helped to inoculate Disraeli against his grandmother's self-hatred and his father's longing to assimilate. It made it possible for him to insist that his Christianity, far from representing a betrayal of his Judaism, was actually an expression of Jewish pride: "I look upon the Church as the only Jewish institution that remains, and, irrespective of its being the depository of divine truth, must ever cling to it as the visible means which embalms the memory of my race."

3

In addition to his baptism, the year 1817 brought two major changes to Disraeli's life. Now that Isaac had inherited his father's fortune, he was able to move the family to a larger house in Bloomsbury, near the British Museum. This would be Disraeli's home base for the next twelve years, until his father quit London for a country estate. At the same time, Ben was now old enough to go away to school. As a Christian, he was no longer disqualified from attending one of the great public schools; Ralph and James, when their time came, would go to Winchester, where they mixed with the children of the aristocracy. But Isaac was not yet confident enough to make such claims for his firstborn son. Instead, Ben was sent to Higham Hall, an obscure school with about fifty students, run by a Unitarian minister whom Isaac had met in a bookstore.

At the very beginning of his career, then, Disraeli was shunted off the path that usually led Englishmen into politics. He received a decent education at Higham Hall, but not a first-class one—as an adult, he was touchy about his limited knowledge of Greek, that badge of a gentleman's education. More important, he missed out on the early connections that sustained many politicians throughout their careers. Nor, when he left school, did he go on to Oxford or Cambridge, where he could have met many of the men who would be his colleagues and rivals in later life. Instead, after less than three years at Higham Hall, Disraeli gave up formal education for good, at the age of fifteen. He spent the next year at home, reading at will in his father's library. Then, in 1821, he was articled to a law firm, where he spent three years training to be an attorney. In the fields that would be most important in his future career—in his knowledge of history, politics, and modern literature—Disraeli was essentially self-educated.

What was it that made him break off his schooling so soon? The only answers, once again, are those he offers in his autobiographical novels, *Vivian Grey* and *Contarini Fleming*. In each of these books, Disraeli's hero starts out as a gifted and charismatic youth, perfectly equipped to succeed in the intensely political atmosphere of a public school. Vivian Grey, Disraeli writes, was "almost better fitted than any young genius whom the playing fields of Eton or the hills of Winton can remember." But like his creator, he is not allowed to attend one of those great schools. Interestingly, Disraeli chalks up this decision to Vivian's overprotective mother, "one of those women whom nothing in the world can persuade that a public school is anything else but a place where boys are roasted alive." Perhaps this was another item on his own bill of grievances against Maria.

Instead, Vivian is sent to a small school run by a Reverend Dallas, where he gets off to a splendid start. He is acclaimed by his classmates as "so dashing! so devilish good-tempered! so completely up to everything!" Yet his very superiority earns him the suspicion and envy of the school's well-born pupils, who abuse him as a "cursed puppy." And the mistrust of the aristocracy turns out to be this parvenu's undoing. Vivian comes up with the idea that the boys should put on a play, even though it is against the school rules. When the teacher, Mr. Mallett, learns of this plan, he lectures the students against following "any seditious stranger," and the word is immediately taken up by Vivian's enemies: " 'No stranger!' shouted St. Leger Smith; 'no stranger!' vociferated a prepared gang." This peculiar insult provokes Vivian to fight back, and Disraeli allows him to wipe the floor with his opponents: "Oh! how beautifully he fought! how admirably straight he hit! and his stops quick as lightning!" But the fight marks the end of Vivian's ascendancy, and within a few pages, after wreaking his revenge on Mallett, he is expelled.

The scant records of Disraeli's childhood make it impossible to say whether this fight scene corresponds to any actual episode. But when we find it reprised, in an even more violent and painful key, in *Contarini Fleming*, there can be no doubt that it expresses some intimate truth about his experience. In the later, more serious novel, published when Disraeli was twenty-seven, the hero once again starts out as a popular schoolboy, admired for his wit: "each word brought forth a new laugh, each sentence of gay nonsense fresh plaudits." Contarini is especially close to a boy he calls Musaeus, with whom he forms a romantic friendship. But he is eventually disillusioned to realize that Musaeus and his other friends are not worthy of his love—that they are actually commonplace boys, while he is a genius. When Contarini's changed attitude toward Musaeus becomes obvious, the rest of the school confronts him, and their "chief" challenges him: "you may think yourself a very great man; but we do not exactly understand the way you are going on."

Soon, as in *Vivian Grey*, the symbolic showdown turns into a fistfight. But this time, Disraeli's description of the combat is no longer slangy and sprightly; it is disturbingly, irrationally violent. Contarini loses control of himself and beats his opponent nearly to death: "I cried out in a voice of madness for him to come on. . . . Each time that he came forward I made the same dreadful spring, beat down his guard, and never ceased working upon his head, until at length my fist seemed to enter his very brain; and after ten rounds he fell down quite blind." Soon afterward, Contarini runs away from school forever.

Superimposing these two episodes, it is hard to avoid the conclusion that in this fight Disraeli is portraying his primal scene, the real or imagined confrontation that defined his first experience of English society outside the family home. He never doubts his own superiority, or his ability to dominate his peers. The danger is, rather, that the very obviousness of his superiority will antagonize his fellows, marking him as a "stranger." What drives both Vivian and Contarini to despair is the recognition that extraordinariness, in a small, homogeneous society (like a school, or a Parliament), does not always bring rewards; sometimes it brings the exact opposite.

The word "Jew" never appears in either of these scenes, or indeed in the novels as a whole. But the experience that Disraeli evokes only really makes sense if it is seen in a Jewish context. Especially in *Vivian Grey*, the shout of "stranger," so odd and uncolloquial, reads like a euphemism for "Jew." The wellborn boys' resentment of Vivian's cleverness, and the schoolmaster's suspicion of his "sedition," chime perfectly with conventional anti-Semitic attitudes. In *Contarini Fleming*, the grievance against Disraeli's hero is his arrogant exclusiveness, a Jewish stereotype that goes back to Shylock—though Contarini's brooding loneliness seems to owe more to Byron than any other example. And the frightening rage he displays in the fistfight reads like the sudden release of a suppressed anger, bred by a long experience of shrugging off insults.

There is every reason to believe that Disraeli's own experience of schoolyard anti-Semitism lies behind these episodes. While there is no record of what went on at Higham Hall, the poet Robert Southey, writing in 1807, left an account of the Jew-baiting he witnessed at another school: "The boys on Easter Sunday rush out of the chapel after school, singing 'He is risen, he is risen,/All the Jews must go to prison.' . . . Some of these boys cut the straps of a Jew's [that is, a Jewish peddler's] box one day, and all his gingerbread nuts fell into the street. Complaint was made to the master, and when he questioned the culprits what they could say in their defense, one of them stepped forward and said, 'Why, sir, did not they crucify our Lord?' " The radical journalist Leigh Hunt recalled the same jingle from his own school days in the 1790s, as well as another: "Get a bit of pork,/Stick it on a fork,/And give it to a Jew boy, a Jew." This kind of folk anti-Semitism seems to have been passed down by generations of children like nursery rhymes, and clearly has little to do with any actual experience of Jews. But when Disraeli was exposed to it, he could not help taking offense, or reacting explosively.

In fact, the crude Jew-baiting that Disraeli encountered as a child did not disappear when he entered the world of politics. *Punch*, the comic magazine that served as a quasi-official chronicle of Victorian political life, was a prime offender in this regard. In 1849, when Disraeli was already a leader of the Conservative Party, *Punch* imagined him singing a ballad:

A Curly-headed Jew-boy some years ago was I,
And through the streets of London "Old Clo" I used
  to cry,
But now I am a Member, I speechifies and votes,
I've given up all my dealin's in left-off hats and coats;
In a creditable manner I hope I fills my sheat,
Though I vonce vos but a Jew-boy vot whistled
  through the street.

Disraeli clearly relished the chance to avenge injuries like this one through Vivian's and Contarini's triumphant violence. But by the time *Punch* made its joke, he had long since learned that showing anger was perfectly counterproductive. "I never trouble to be avenged," he said late in life, "but, when a man injures me, I put his name on a slip of paper and lock it up in a drawer. It is marvellous how men I have thus labelled have a knack of disappearing." Only once, early in his career, did Disraeli actually threaten the kind of violence that Contarini committed, when he challenged a politician who had used anti-Semitic language to a duel. As he got older, Disraeli learned to manage his temper with rigid self-control, deliberately cultivating an air of ironic detachment. His reputation as a parliamentary debater rested on this mocking coolness, which he used to make his more passionate opponents look ridiculous. During an 1871 debate on foreign policy, when Gladstone as prime minister faced Disraeli as leader of the Opposition, one observer noted: "The Premier was like a cat on hot bricks, and presented a striking contrast to Disraeli; for Disraeli cuts up a Minister with as much *sang-froid* as an anatomist cuts up a frog." It is only by reading his early novels that we can see how hard he had to work to earn that sangfroid.

For all the obstacles he faced, however, there is no doubt that the young Disraeli was born to a position that most Englishmen would have envied. During his years as a student and law clerk, in fact, Britain was passing through one of the most turbulent periods in its modern history. In 1815, the country celebrated the final defeat of Napoléon, after more than twenty years of continual warfare with France. But the adjustment to peacetime brought a whole new set of problems. In particular, the collapse of agricultural prices, after many years without competition from Continental farmers, caused severe distress among the landowners who dominated Parliament. Their response was to enact the Corn Laws, which placed tariffs on imported grain in order to keep domestic prices artificially high. This protectionist measure benefited landowners at the direct expense of city-dwellers, who ended up paying more for food.

For three decades, the Corn Laws—whose actual effect on prices historians continue to debate—were crucially important as a symbolic issue. By taking from the city to give to the country, they stood as a constant reminder of the landowners' monopoly of political power, and the disenfranchisement of the middle class, industrial workers, and the growing northern cities. The fight over the Corn Laws, and with them England's traditional class structure, was one of the great ideological battles of the early Victorian period. It was his role in this debate, as a champion of the most conservative and protectionist faction in Parliament, that would elevate Disraeli to the first rank in British politics.

The fight over the Corn Laws became more and more bitter as the Industrial Revolution, combined with an unprecedented population explosion, made life harder for England's urban and rural poor. As the population of Britain climbed, from twelve million in 1811 to twenty-one million in 1851, the country struggled to find new ways of dealing with poverty, unemployment, illiteracy, child labor, and pollution. Even as Britain as a whole grew richer—leading the world in industry and commerce, railroads and shipbuilding—the emergence of a permanent underclass shocked the conscience of the country. Almost all of the great Victorian writers, from Carlyle and Ruskin to Dickens and George Eliot, were in fact critics of Victorian society, pointing out its huge disparities of wealth, its callous neglect of the poor, its Philistine materialism. Here, too, Disraeli would play a central role: in his novel *Sybil*, he invented the concept of "The Two Nations"—the rich and the poor—that would help to shape Victorian thinking about social justice.

All these economic and social anxieties helped to fuel serious political agitation. The worst moment came in 1819, when a protest meeting at St. Peter's Fields, outside Manchester, was attacked by soldiers, causing eleven deaths and hundreds of injuries. The "Peterloo Massacre," as it was called in mocking reference to the British triumph at Waterloo, looked to English radicals like a summons to revolution. The mood was captured by Percy Bysshe Shelley in one of the best protest poems ever written, "England in 1819":

> An old, mad, blind, despised, and dying king,—
> Princes, the dregs of their dull race, who flow
> Through public scorn,—mud from a muddy spring,—
> Rulers who neither see, nor feel, nor know,
> But leech-like to their fainting country cling,

Till they drop, blind in blood, without a blow,—
A people starved and stabbed in the untilled field,—
An army, which liberticide and prey
Makes as a two-edged sword to all who wield,—
Golden and sanguine laws which tempt and slay;
Religion Christless, Godless—a book sealed;
A Senate,—Time's worst statute unrepealed,—
Are graves, from which a glorious Phantom may
Burst, to illumine our tempestuous day.

When Shelley described Parliament as "Time's worst statute unrepealed," he was articulating the central political grievance of the period. Britain's electoral system had barely been altered since the Revolution of 1688, even as the demographics of the country were transformed. In the early 1830s, out of a population of more than 16 million, only five hundred thousand men had the right to vote. To make matters worse, many of the boroughs that sent members to Parliament were not just unrepresentative but corrupt, their voters bought or bullied by a local magnate. Even after the worst abuses were remedied by the Reform Bill of 1832, the expansion of the franchise would remain a major issue in Victorian politics.

The political and social problems that were to shape Disraeli's career, then, were already becoming acute during his early years. But even as a teenager, Disraeli was not inclined to be meekly grateful for his class privileges, or anxious about losing them. That sort of bourgeois conservatism never appealed to him, and he would never display the virtues and vices of the bourgeoisie—thrift and timidity, earnestness and hardheartedness. His conservative philosophy was of another sort—romantic and in some ways radical, a matter not of defending the status quo but of regenerating English society in accordance with its best traditions.

This meant that Disraeli's imaginative peers, from the beginning, were the upper class, the men born to rule. All the brilliant incongruities of his life and career stem from this fundamental anomaly. Born to a middle-class family, living in a period that exalted middle-class virtues, Disraeli was an aristocrat at heart. His lifestyle, his novels, his politics, and his thinking about Judaism can all be understood as gambits to convince the world, and himself, that the aristocracy was where he belonged.

And compared to a real son of the nobility, if not to the average English farmer or worker, Disraeli did start life at a disadvantage. His education was both a product and a marker of his socially marginal origins, and its effects can be seen all through his career. He did manage, against all odds, to reach what he called "the top of the greasy pole" of politics. But the climb was very long, and for many years he could only watch as better-connected men passed him by. It took Disraeli five tries before he succeeded in getting elected to Parliament; once he did, it was fifteen years before he first held office.

To see how much smoother the path to power could be for

a young man from the right background, it is only necessary to look at the early years of Gladstone, in so many ways Disraeli's perfect foil. Technically, Gladstone, too, was born into the middle class. But while his father did not have a title, he had something just as good—an immense fortune, earned through trade with the West Indies, where he owned a large number of slaves. Gladstone senior sat in Parliament, and he sent his son William Ewart to the very best schools in the country—first Eton, then Christ Church, Oxford. When Gladstone was twenty-one years old, he gave a speech at the Oxford Union that caused such a sensation word of it reached the Duke of Newcastle, a major political figure. The duke—encouraged by his son, who was Gladstone's friend and classmate—offered the rising star a seat in Parliament whenever he was ready to take it. The next year, Gladstone accepted the offer; the duke and his father split the considerable expenses of the campaign; and in 1832, at the age of twenty-two, he entered the House of Commons. Though five years younger than Disraeli, Gladstone got into Parliament five years earlier. For the next half-century, the contest between Gladstone the earnest Christian and Disraeli the untrustworthy Jew would help to define Victorian political life.

4

If anyone had offered Disraeli a seat in the House of Commons when he was twenty-two, there is no doubt he would have leapt at the chance. Because he became an author so young, it is natural to assume that literature, rather than politics, was Disraeli's first vocation. Certainly he was famous as a novelist long before he achieved comparable success as a politician. But in fact, Disraeli wrote his first novel, *Vivian Grey*, only after the failure of his first political project, and the best parts of the book are directly based on that debacle. Though he would continue to write fiction, at intervals, throughout his life, his chief ambition was always for himself, never for his art. When he asked, in a later novel, "Would you rather have been Homer or Julius Caesar, Shakespeare or Napoleon? No one doubts," he meant that he could not imagine anyone choosing the men of thought over the men of action. "A man of great energies," he believed, "aspires that they should be felt in his lifetime, that his existence should be rendered more intensely vital by the constant consciousness of his multiplied and multiplying power." It is no wonder, then, that Disraeli's fiction is at its best when he deals with the world of power, using the medium of the novel to advance his own political prospects and ideas.

Politics was already on Disraeli's mind when, just before his seventeenth birthday, his father sent him to work at a London law firm. "I had some scruples" about this plan, Disraeli later recalled, "for even then I dreamed of Parliament." For the next two and a half years, while he continued to live at home, he worked as a clerk, ostensibly preparing himself to join the bar. But he quickly decided that the greatest glory he could hope for as a lawyer—and he always assumed that the greatest was his destiny—was not glorious enough. "The Bar: pooh!" thinks Vivian Grey. "Law and bad jokes till we are forty; and then, with the most brilliant success, the prospect of gout and a coronet . . . to be a great lawyer, I must give up my chance of being a great man."

Rather than give up that chance, Disraeli gave up the law. In July 1824, he left work to go on a tour of Germany with his father, and by the time he returned he had very different plans. Britain had recently recognized the independence of the new Latin American republics, and the stock market responded by rapidly inflating the prices of South American mining stocks. Disraeli, like many others, saw a chance to make his fortune, and in partnership with two friends, he invested heavily in mining companies. When the government, recognizing a bubble in the making, began to caution investors, Disraeli was hired by a stock-promoter to write pamphlets attacking the government and praising South American mines as good investments.

But Disraeli's *An Enquiry into the Plans, Progress, and Policy of the American Mining Companies*—a more dignified nineteenth-century equivalent of stock promotion spam—

could not change the laws of economics. By the middle of 1825 the bubble burst, leaving him thousands of pounds in the red. This was the beginning of what eventually grew into a mountain of debt, as Disraeli kept borrowing from moneylenders at high rates of interest. By the 1830s, he was regularly dodging bailiffs sent by his creditors to arrest him. His novel writing descended into hackwork, as he tried to keep afloat by turning out book after book. Not until the end of that decade—when he got into Parliament, making himself immune to arrest, and married a rich woman— would Disraeli escape the threat of jail.

Even then, his debts remained a serious political embarrassment. In 1841, when Disraeli was running for reelection to Parliament, his opponents plastered the town of Shrewsbury with a poster listing fifteen court judgments against him, for a total—printed in big block letters—of "Twenty-two Thousand and Thirty-six Pounds, Two Shillings, and Eleven Pence." "Honest Electors of Shrewsbury!" the poster shrilled. "Will you be represented by such a man? Can you confide in his pledges?"

But if Disraeli's recklessness saddled him with debts, his genius helped him to turn his debts into a kind of imaginative asset. "If youth but knew the fatal misery that they are entailing on themselves the moment they accept a pecuniary credit to which they are not entitled, how they would start in their career! how pale they would turn! how they would tremble, and clasp their hands in agony at the precipice on which they are disporting!" So Disraeli writes in *Henrietta*

Temple, a novel whose hero, Ferdinand Armine, finds his marriage plans thwarted by his debts. Yet it is not hard to sense the hyperbole, the comic gusto, in that lamentation. Being in debt, Disraeli seems to say, is fatal but not serious.

Elsewhere, he writes about debt with positive affection. "I should be incapable of anything, if it were not for my debts," jokes a character in *Tancred*. "I am naturally so indolent, that if I did not remember in the morning that I was ruined, I should never be able to distinguish myself." And Disraeli did seem to draw a kind of nervous stimulation from being in such dire straits. Still more important, being in debt was a very aristocratic predicament. The heir who borrows heavily against his inheritance was a familiar figure in both life and literature. Not to let sordid financial concerns interfere with one's pleasures and entitlements was a badge of the nobleman, especially in a society increasingly dominated by bourgeois, mercantile values. In his fascinating diary, Lord Stanley, the son of Disraeli's colleague the Earl of Derby, worried about this tendency among his class: "The truth is, fashionable society discourages and ridicules any man who looks after his affairs, while it has a very strong sympathy with those who have ruined themselves, no matter how much by their own fault. A certain contempt of economy and prudence has always been characteristic of an aristocracy."

To Disraeli, who was precociously alert to the values of the aristocracy, it might even have seemed better to be in debt than to be too scrupulous about money. This was especially the case for a socially ambitious Jew. For he could not have failed to observe that the moneylenders to whom improvident young lords applied were stereotypically Jewish. "Going to the Jews" was practically a synonym for borrowing money; one of the categories listed on the election poster of Disraeli's creditors, along with "Tailors, Hosiers, Upholsterers," was "Jew Money Lenders."

Disraeli reflected this reality in *Henrietta Temple*. When Ferdinand Armine goes borrowing, the first place he tries is the firm of "Messrs. Morris and Levison," whose names make clear that they are Jewish. Disraeli does not portray Levison as a villain, a modern-day Shylock. He is merely vulgar, as we can see by his dress: "He wore a plum-coloured frock coat of the finest cloth; his green velvet waistcoat was guarded by a gold chain, which would have been the envy of a new town council; an immense opal gleamed on the breast of his embroidered shirt; and his fingers were covered with very fine rings." Later, when Ferdinand is arrested for debt and confined to a "sponging-house"—a sort of hotel, run by moneylenders, where debtors could try to make arrangements for payment before they went to jail—he notices that the drawing room features "some sources of literary amusement . . . in the shape of a Hebrew Bible and the Racing Calendar."

Disraeli's detailed description of Levison's office, right down to the interior decoration, strongly suggests that he knew a few such moneylenders firsthand. He may even have spent time in a sponging-house, though the record is not clear. Such experiences would only have confirmed that, if he had to be identified with either the Jewish creditors or the noble debtors, he would prefer the latter. Being in debt, like almost everything in Disraeli's life, was both an expression of his aristocratic self-image and an instrument in its creation.

And even though he was barely out of his teens, Disraeli was already beginning to create the image that would make him one of the most recognizable, and most caricatured, men in England. Disraeli's name is forever associated with the Victorian era: he was first elected to Parliament in the year Victoria came to the throne, and to the end of his life he never served another monarch. But it is important to remember that his personal style was formed under the more raffish dispensation of the Regency, a time when English society was highly receptive to eccentrics, dandies, and geniuses. The presiding genius of the period was Lord Byron, who scandalized and titillated the English with his sexual adventures and self-mythologizing poems. His death in 1824 seemed even at the time to mark the dimming of a more colorful and vivid age. Edward Bulwer-Lytton, the novelist-politician who became Disraeli's friend in the late 1820s, lamented "that strong attachment to the Practical, which became so visible a little time after the death of Byron."

Disraeli, however, kept faith with the values of Byronism. While he never met Byron in person, his father did—Byron, as we have seen, admired Isaac's work—and as a teenager he heard inside gossip about the poet from Murray. After his death, Disraeli developed a positive cult of Byron: he sought out people who had known him, visited the places mentioned in his poems, and even wrote a novel, *Venetia*, based on his life. At one point Disraeli tried to rent the rooms Byron had occupied in the fashionable Albany apartments, and he actually did manage to hire Byron's Italian manservant and bring him back to England.

More important, Disraeli modeled his own image on the great man's, imitating his flamboyant dress and his haughty, world-weary expression. He got the effect perfectly, as we can see from an eyewitness description of Disraeli on the hustings in 1835: "There was a sort of half-smile, half-sneer, playing about his beautifully-formed mouth, the upper lip of which was curved as we see it in the portraits of Byron. . . . He was very showily attired in a dark bottle-green frock-coat, a waistcoat of the most extravagant pattern, the front of which was almost covered with glittering chains, and in fancy-pattern pantaloons. . . . Altogether he was the most intellectual-looking exquisite I had ever seen."

His "exquisite" appearance, combined with his precocious genius and sharp wit, helped ease Disraeli's way into London society. It also made him very attractive to women—especially the older, married, but still available women who played such an important behind-the-scenes role in English political life. Before his marriage, Disraeli conducted a series of affairs with such women, entering eagerly into a dissolute aristocratic milieu where politics and adultery were overlapping pastimes. To the end of his life, he credited his mistresses, and the many other women whom he merely charmed, with helping to make his career possible. "Few great men have flourished," he wrote in *Henrietta Temple*, "who, were they candid, would not acknowledge the vast advantages they have experienced in the earlier years of their career from the spirit and sympathy of woman."

With youth, talent, and good looks all in his favor, Disraeli was not about to let his stock market reverses discourage him. He was too busy working on a new scheme, which promised to bring him not just profits but political influence. Since childhood, he had been acquainted with his father's publisher, John Murray, the owner of the influential Tory magazine, the *Quarterly Review*. Murray had printed Disraeli's mining pamphlets on commission, and was himself speculating in South American shares. In the summer of 1825, Murray, Disraeli, and another of their stock market partners agreed to launch a major new business: a daily newspaper, intended as a liberal Tory alternative to the *Times*.

It is not clear exactly how Disraeli was expected to come up with his share of the funds for this very expensive venture. But he did contribute the new paper's name, the *Representative*, and he plunged into the business of hiring staff and lining up foreign correspondents. Murray sent him to Scotland to try to convince J. G. Lockhart, an eminent man of letters and Sir Walter Scott's son-in-law, to serve as the paper's editor. Lockhart was bemused by his visitor's extreme youth—he seems to have expected Isaac D'Israeli, not Benjamin—and the negotiations got off to a rocky start. Disraeli, however, was having the time of his life. At last, he was involved in the kind of intrigue he had dreamed about. He even wrote letters to Murray in code, as though he were a secret agent, intimating that highly placed Tory politicians were in his pocket.

Lockhart, however, was not won over by these grand hints and promises. Worse, as the stock market crashed and banks began to fail, it became clear that Disraeli would never be able to come up with his portion of the capital for what Isaac called "the new intellectual Steam Engine." By the time the paper launched, in January 1826, Disraeli was no longer involved. It turned out to be just as well: the *Representative* was a failure, and stopped publishing after just six months.

Disraeli had been out in the world for less than a year, and already he had two major reverses to his account. But he was still not discouraged, and he immediately found a way to turn his experiences with Murray to good use. As Disraeli knew, the literary event of 1825 was *Tremaine, or the Man of Refinement*, a novel by Robert Plumer Ward. It was the first novel to claim to describe the manners of high society accurately, from the inside, and it helped launch the genre of so-called silver fork fiction. The fact that *Tremaine* was published anonymously only heightened its credibility, and its allure: readers had the impression that a spy was sending them reports from deep inside the aristocracy.

Disraeli decided to capitalize on this trend, and within months of leaving the *Representative*, writing at top speed, he produced the first volume of *Vivian Grey*. He sent the manuscript to Sara Austen, an acquaintance of Isaac's who had served as Ward's literary agent, and she agreed to perform the same service for Disraeli. Sara, it seems, was the first in the line of older women who were smitten with Disraeli. Though they were probably not lovers, she devoted herself wholeheartedly to advancing his career; and thanks to her good offices, Colburn, the publisher of *Tremaine*, agreed to bring out *Vivian Grey* in the spring of 1826. The author's identity would be kept a secret; even the publisher didn't know it, communicating with Disraeli only through Sara.

Perhaps if Colburn had known that his author was actually a twenty-one-year-old Jew, whose knowledge of high society began and ended at his father's dinner table, he wouldn't have publicized *Vivian Grey* quite so aggressively as a scandalous tell-all. Items planted in newspapers suggested that the novel would contain "portraits of living characters, sufficient to constitute a National Gallery," and keys were circulated linking the characters to their putative originals. All this speculation helped to make *Vivian Grey* a sensation.

The plot of the novel is loosely based on the intrigues surrounding the *Representative*, transposed from journalism to politics. Vivian, Disraeli's impudent, ambitious stand-in, schemes to organize a new political party, with the aim of installing the mediocre Marquess of Carabas as prime minister. By flattering Carabas's senile conceit, Vivian establishes himself as the real power behind the throne and convinces his patron to seek an alliance with Frederick Cleveland, his old political rival. But after some ludicrous romantic byplay, featuring a temptress and poisoner named Mrs. Felix Lorraine, the faction Vivian has assembled falls apart. Carabas's hopes of office are disappointed, and Cleveland ends up challenging Vivian to a duel ("Out upon your honied words and your soft phrases! I have been their dupe too long!"). Our hero tries to fire in the air, but when Cleveland insists on exchanging shots, Vivian unintentionally kills him.

Only those deeply in the know could have identified the slender factual basis for this extravagant story. Murray, for one, instantly recognized himself in Carabas, Vivian's vain dupe, and accused his former protégé of an "outrageous breach of all confidence and of every tie which binds man to man." But neither Carabas nor Cleveland, who stands in for Lockhart, is drawn finely enough to make their originals detectable. The only person who really stands revealed in *Vivian Grey* is the author, and he is so starkly exposed that the book is almost embarrassing to read.

Vivian has all of his creator's charm, arrogance, and vaulting ambition, without any ballast of scruple or political principle. Even as a teenager, he dreams of nothing but power: "He paced his chamber in an agitated spirit, and panted for the Senate." But Disraeli had neither the worldly experience nor the knowledge of human nature to understand what the practice of politics is really like. Instead, he imagines Vivian as a sublime confidence man, merely pretending to care about the people he means to exploit. "Yes! we must mix with the herd," he reflects; "we must enter into their feelings; we must humour their weaknesses; we must sympathise with the sorrows that we do not feel; and share the merriment of fools."

Vivian, it appears, would do absolutely anything to get ahead. He even jokes that he would sell his soul: "What a pity, Miss Manvers, the fashion has gone out of selling oneself to the devil." This cynical, world-weary tone makes Disraeli sound like an ancestor of Oscar Wilde, and it is impossible to appreciate *Vivian Grey* without enjoying his boyish pleasure in outraging the pieties. But Disraeli is not simply joking when he imagines Vivian's political career as a devil's bargain. "Think you not," Vivian says, "that intellect is as much a purchasable article as fine parks and fair castles?" He resolves to sell his talents to the aristocracy in exchange for a place among them: "At this moment, how many a powerful noble wants only wit to be a Minister; and what wants Vivian Grey to attain the same end? That noble's influence. When two persons can so materially assist each other, why are they not brought together? Shall I, because my birth baulks my fancy, shall I pass my life a moping misanthrope in an old chateau?"

In this passage, we hear the voice of Vivian's creator with painful clarity. Disraeli had already learned, at twenty-one, what it meant to have his birth balk his fancy. As a Jew, he recognized, the road to power was practically closed to him. But he also knew that he had extraordinary talents, and he couldn't tolerate the possibility that he would never get a chance to use them. The most authentic note in Disraeli's early fiction is the way he describes the unbearable pain of frustrated ambition. His dominant emotion in these years was the one he evoked in his second novel, *The Young Duke:*

> View the obscure Napoleon starving in the streets of Paris. What was St. Helena to the bitterness of such existence? The visions of past glory might illumine even that dark imprisonment; but to be conscious that his supernatural energies might die away without creating their miracles: can the wheel or the rack rival the torture of such a suspicion?

The problem for Disraeli would be to ensure that his extraordinariness did not work against him. He would need to find sponsors in the political establishment, and he would need to earn their trust without forfeiting their respect. Writing *Vivian Grey* allowed Disraeli to clarify and dramatize these challenges. But publishing it, as he should have been able to predict, only made them more difficult. By creating Vivian, Disraeli gave the impression that he, too, was unprincipled, an intellectual mercenary, ready to cut a deal with anyone rich or powerful enough to serve his purposes. For the rest of his career, his enemies called him a hypocrite, and his friends worried that the charge might be true.

Vivian Grey would not make such uncomfortable reading, even today, were it not for the fact that Disraeli's subsequent career closely followed Vivian's prescription. For Disraeli rose to power by making his intelligence available to "the stupid party," as John Stuart Mill dubbed the Conservatives, just as Vivian sold his intellect to the dull-witted Carabas. He led the Conservatives in the House of Commons not because they loved him—in fact, most of them distrusted and resented him—but because he was indispensable, their only man of genius. One Conservative MP made the situation clear with a cricket metaphor: "We know he does not belong to our eleven, but we have him down as a professional bowler." This is the tragic element in Disraeli's career: even at the height of his power, even among his closest allies, he remained an outsider. And it was his Jewishness, that irreducible otherness, that made it impossible for him to close the gap.

In 1826, however, the psychological implications of *Vivian Grey* were less important to Disraeli than the angry backlash it provoked. Much of the novel's cocky charm comes from its affectation of familiarity with elegant society, and its pages crawl with noblemen and millionaires. ("Mr. Puff, allow me to introduce you to Lord Alhambra," runs a typical line of dialogue.) But as word of the author's true identity leaked out, readers began to feel that they had been duped, and the critics turned vicious. *Blackwood's Magazine* wrote that the anonymous author was actually "an obscure person, for whom nobody cares a straw," while the *Magnet* called Disraeli "a swindler—a scoundrel—a liar," and threatened that "several horsewhips were preparing for him."

In less than two years, Disraeli had failed to make a fortune on the stock market and failed to gain political power with his newspaper. Now his attempt to win literary fame had ended in disgrace. As he would write a few years later, remembering this episode in *Contarini Fleming:* "With what horror, with what blank despair, with what supreme, appalling astonishment, did I find myself, for the first time in my life, a subject of the most reckless, the most malignant, and the most adroit ridicule. I was sacrificed, I was scalped. . . . I felt that sickness of heart, which we experience in our first serious scrape. I was ridiculous. It was time to die."

5

But Disraeli didn't die; instead, he had a nervous breakdown. While the furor over *Vivian Grey* cooled, Disraeli took a two-month trip to Europe, in the company of Sara Austen and her husband. The group went through France to Switzerland, then over the Alps into northern Italy, all of which Disraeli described in picturesque letters home. When he returned to England in the fall, he completed a second installment of *Vivian Grey*, a largely forgettable book that gives every sign of having been written for money. The psychological self-portrait of the first volume gives way to a disconnected series of fairy-tale episodes, and Vivian is just a shadow of his former self. The contrast is so striking that even the author asks, "Could he really be the same individual as the daring youth who then organized the crazy councils of those ambitious, imbecile grey-beards?"

He wasn't, and neither was his creator. For the next three years, Disraeli was a semi-invalid, suffering from one of those indefinable nineteenth-century illnesses that now look obviously psychosomatic. He retreated to his family home, allowing his parents to look after him as he underwent treatment at the hands of a series of helpless doctors. The best medical opinion he could find was that he had "chronic inflammation of the membranes of the brain," but today he would probably be diagnosed with acute depression. Disraeli was never totally inactive, and he even managed to produce two minor works: *Popanilla*, a short satire in the vein of *Gulliver's Travels*, appeared in 1828, and *The Young Duke* was finished by 1830. But compared to the whirlwind of planning and plotting in 1824–26, the years 1827–30 appear, as Isaac said, like "a blank" in his son's life. "His complaint," Isaac recognized, "is one of those perplexing cases which remain uncertain and obscure, till they are finally got rid of. Meanwhile patience and resignation must be his lot—two drugs in human life, bitter of digestion, in an ardent and excitable mind."

In fact, Isaac knew just what his son was suffering, since he had been through the same thing himself. At the age of twenty-nine, according to Disraeli's memorial essay, "there came over my father that mysterious illness to which the youth of men of sensibility, and especially literary men, is frequently subject—a failing of nervous energy, occasioned by study and too sedentary habits, early and habitual reverie, restless and indefinite purpose. The symptoms, physical and moral, are most distressing: lassitude and despondency." Disraeli is surely describing his own "mysterious illness" here as well, and the cause he suggests for Isaac's depression is even more applicable to his own case: "I should think that this illness of his youth, and which, though of a fitful character, was of many years' duration, arose from his inability to direct to a satisfactory end the intellectual power which he was conscious of possessing."

The pain of thwarted ambition was the root cause of Disraeli's three-year illness. He had started his career under a serious narcissistic delusion, as *Vivian Grey* ingenuously reveals. Convinced of his own genius, he believed that the world would acclaim it as well, and instantly yield him the supremacy he deserved. When this failed to happen, the self-image he had nurtured, through years of baiting by his schoolmates and solitary dreaming in his father's library, was shattered. In time, Disraeli would manage to repair his self-confidence and place it on a firmer foundation. Indeed, he would manage to accomplish everything Vivian dreamed of, and more.

But there remains, throughout his career, a lingering sense of disappointment—a suggestion that power and fame, because they came late and with effort, could never live up to his expectation. "To be famous when you are young is the fortune of the gods," Disraeli wrote, and he filled his work with catalogues of young heroes: "Why, the greatest captains of ancient and modern times both conquered Italy at five-and-twenty! Youth, extreme youth overthrew the Persian Empire. . . . Cortes was little more than thirty when he gazed upon the golden cupolas of Mexico." Like Julius Caesar weeping before the statue of Alexander, the young Disraeli was tormented by the thought of how little he had managed to accomplish. When he did finally gain real power, he was an old man, and he could not banish the sense that it had come too late. "There were days when, on waking, I felt I could move dynasties and governments," he said in 1878, "but that has passed away."

B y 1830, Disraeli's health and spirits had begun to recover enough to make him eager for a change. One sign of the improvement, or perhaps the cause of it, was that he embarked on his first recorded love affair—ironically enough, with the wife of one of his doctors, Clara Bolton. Clara, like Sara Austen, was older and married, both qualities he looked for in his mistresses. It couldn't have hurt her appeal to the ambitious young man that she was also a fashionable hostess, whose guests included members of Parliament. Disraeli had gradually been reentering society, dividing his time between London, where he flaunted his clothes and dodged his creditors, and Bradenham, his father's new country house in Buckinghamshire, where the family had moved in search of healthier surroundings.

Now Disraeli yearned for travel. But he did not plan a conventional Grand Tour, of the kind that took rich young Englishmen to the salons of Paris and the churches of Rome. Instead, he planned to go to the East—to Greece, Turkey, Egypt, and the Holy Land. In this, too, he was following his idol's example. Byron had died in Greece, fighting in that country's war of independence, and some of his most popular works were highly colored tales of the East, full of primitive, unrestrained passions.

But for Disraeli, a journey to the East had a symbolic dimension it could not have offered Byron: it meant coming face-to-face with the homeland of the Jews. Visiting Palestine would not be a religious pilgrimage for Disraeli. His secular upbringing and Christian baptism meant that he was not steeped in the Jewish liturgy, with its constant evocations of Zion and Jerusalem. But it was precisely because Disraeli did not view Palestine religiously, as the stage for a messianic drama of exile and redemption, that he was able to imagine it in historical and political terms, as a site of Jewish national sovereignty. Reading in his father's library, he had recently become intrigued by the figure of David Alroy, a twelfth-century Kurdish Jew who led a rebellion against the Seljuk Turks. For Disraeli, Alroy represented a previously undreamt-of possibility: that a Jew could claim political power as a Jew. More than the promise of a warm climate, more than Byron's example, it was this dream—which had not yet been named Zionism—that drew Disraeli to the East.

In May 1830, with his fee for *The Young Duke* in his pocket, Disraeli left London. His traveling companion was William Meredith, the fiancé of his sister, Sarah; later the two of them joined up with another friend, James Clay, who was touring the Mediterranean in his yacht. Clay's presence was a hint that there was more than sightseeing on the agenda: he was a notorious libertine, making him a perfect guide to the kind of sex tourism that drew young Westerners to the East. Disraeli did not leave a salacious account of his sexual experiences, as Gustave Flaubert did when he traveled much the same route twenty years later. But the fact that, on their return to England, both Disraeli and Clay were treated for venereal disease makes their activities abroad sufficiently clear. Indeed, in the right company, Disraeli seems to have been happy to talk about his sexual adventures. In 1833, the painter Benjamin Haydon wrote in his diary about a dinner party where Disraeli "talked much of the East, and seemed tinged with a disposition to palliate its infamous vices."

Disraeli's first stop was Gibraltar, where his Byronic dress and manner dazzled the British garrison. At least, that is the impression he was keen to give in his letters home: "I have also the fame of being the first who ever passed the Straits with two canes, a morning and an evening cane. . . . It is wonderful the effect these magical wands produce." Later, he gave his foppishness an Eastern twist, decking himself out in "the costume of a Greek pirate. A blood red shirt with silver studs as big as shillings, an immense scarf or girdle full of pistols and daggers, a red cap, red slippers, blue broad striped jacket and trousers. Excessively wicked!"

But Disraeli's choice of clothes had to do with more than just his love of playing dress-up. It was a way of acknowledging, by exaggerating, his inability to blend into the crowd. How far he carried this effort can be seen in a letter from Malta, where he socialized with British officers: "Affectation tells here even better than wit. Yesterday, at the racket court, sitting in the gallery among strangers, the ball entered, lightly struck me, and fell at my feet. I picked it up, and observing a young rifleman excessively stiff, I humbly requested him to forward its passage into the court, as I really had never thrown a ball in my life." It was a joke that might have gone over well with his friends in London, where such dandyism and preciousness was in vogue.

But there is also no mistaking the defensiveness of Disraeli's gesture. Knowing how far he must remain from the ideal of an officer and a gentleman, he refuses to make the slightest effort in that direction; he won't even try to throw a ball. Disraeli must have known, whatever he claimed in his letter, that such "affectation" would not "tell" very far with the Malta garrison, and Clay confirms that it did not. Looking back on the trip years later, he described Disraeli's "coxcombry" as "insupportable," and recalled that the officers soon stopped inviting "that damned bumptious Jew boy" to dinner in the mess. But his extreme dandyism, in Malta as in England, served Disraeli's most intimate need. It allowed him to feel that his extraordinariness was a matter of choice, and therefore a kind of virtue, rather than a matter of birth, and therefore a curse. As always, if he could not fit in, he was determined to stand out.

But if Disraeli felt compelled to play the fool among Englishmen, his travels gave him the chance to escape into a freer and more dignified imaginative atmosphere. He was delighted, for instance, when the old woman who guided him around the Alhambra, the grand Islamic palace in Granada, kept asking if he was a Moor. The notion that his Mediterranean features, which marked him as an inferior back home, might be taken as a sign of nobility abroad was greatly stimulating to his imagination. Perhaps he was already constructing the historically dubious, psychologically potent theory that Jews and Arabs were racially identical, so that the glories of both peoples could be claimed by the members of each—the idea that, as he put it in *Tancred*, "The Arabs are only Jews upon horseback." At any rate, he reveled in the notion that he might be a legitimate heir to the princes who built the Alhambra. Leaving the palace, he was heard to murmur, "*Es mi casa*," "This is my house."

The allure of power to the powerless also helps to explain why Disraeli immediately fell in love with the Turks. For a disciple of Byron, this was a surprising heresy. After all, the poet had died fighting for the Greeks against Turkey; for liberals across Europe, the Ottoman Empire was a symbol of decadence and reaction. But when Disraeli reached Albania, where a rebellion was raging, he instantly took the side of the Turkish overlords. "I had some thoughts," he wrote home, "indeed had resolved, to join the Turkish Army as volunteer in the Albanian war." As in Spain, he reveled in the chance to escape Englishness and mingle with what he could imagine as a powerful Semitic race. For while the Turks were not in fact Semites, the Ottoman Empire was home to a large Sephardic community, descendants of the same Spanish diaspora to which Disraeli traced his own origins. It would only have taken a slight turn of fate's wheel to make him a Turkish gentleman instead of an English one, and he was delighted when one Turk he met "told me that he did not think I was an Englishman because I walked so slow: in fact I find the habits of this calm and luxurious people entirely agree with my own preconceived opinions of propriety and enjoyment, and I detest the Greeks more than ever."

The Greek rebellion may not have been the idealistic struggle for freedom that it became in the hands of the Romantic poets. But Disraeli's contempt for the Greeks, and for every subsequent struggle for national liberation in the nineteenth century, points to what would become the most troubling aspect of his imagination of power. Disraeli felt drawn to Islamic power, in Spain and Turkey, because he experienced it as a surrogate for Jewish power. In his mind, the evident grandeur of the Moors and Turks served as a rebuke to the haughtiness of the English, proving how much an Eastern, Semitic people could accomplish. Again and again in his fiction, he delighted in contrasting the antiquity of the Semite with the immaturity of the Anglo-Saxon— "some flat-nosed Frank, full of bustle and puffed up with self-conceit," as he wrote in *Tancred*, "a race spawned perhaps in the morasses of some Northern forest hardly yet cleared."

Yet this method of bolstering his Jewish pride compelled Disraeli to overlook the fact that, in reality, the Jews had much more in common with the Greeks than with the Turks. In the nineteenth century, the Jews were not an imperial people but a subject one, and their plight was especially bad in the Ottoman Empire. Just ten years after Disraeli's journey, in 1840, the blood libel resurfaced in Damascus, where the murder of a Catholic priest was blamed on a Jewish barber. The resulting campaign of terror led to the torture of the city's leading Jews, several of whom died. Only the intervention of Western diplomats, prodded by the prominent English Jew Moses Montefiore, forced the Egyptian government of Mehemet Ali to put a stop to the Damascus Affair.

Ironically, meeting Mehemet Ali had been one of the highlights of Disraeli's Eastern tour. He was dazzled by the pasha's "court, a very brilliant circle, in most gorgeous dresses, particularly the black eunuchs in scarlet and gold." He even claimed, improbably, that Mehemet Ali discussed politics with him. Yet for Disraeli to admire the pasha as a symbol of Semitic power, he had to ignore the fact that that power was exercised at the expense of his own people, the Jews. Indeed, Disraeli did not join in Montefiore's campaign to save the Jews of Damascus, even though he was by then a member of Parliament. It was a telling example of the way Disraeli, while imagining Jewishness in ways that were psychologically empowering, paid little attention to the condition of actually existing Jewry. This elevation of his fantasy of Jewishness over the political reality of the Jews of his time is why Disraeli belongs to the prehistory of Zionism, rather than Zionism proper.

Given how intensively Disraeli was thinking about Jewish history during his trip, we might expect his letters from Palestine to be full of epiphanies. In fact, while he says that his visit to Jerusalem was "the most delightful of all our travels," his descriptions of the city are disappointing. He waxes conventionally eloquent about the landscape— "Nothing could be conceived more wild, and terrible, and desolate than the surrounding scenery, more dark, and stormy, and severe"—and his letters remain on the level of tourism. Perhaps he did not dwell further on the reality of Palestine because, at the time of his visit, it did not present a very convincing picture of Jewish grandeur. On the two-day journey from the port of Jaffa to Jerusalem, Disraeli would have had to ride on horseback over roads too rough to accommodate carriages, while paying bribes to a series of local chieftains. Jerusalem itself had just thirteen thousand inhabitants, of whom perhaps five thousand were Jews; it had not yet expanded beyond its medieval walls, and looked less like an ancient capital than a shabby provincial town. An English minister who visited the city in 1849 wrote that Jerusalem struck him as "unpleasant and disagreeably dirty . . . the traveller . . . has to make his way as best he can amid loose stones, dirt and nastiness."

It may be precisely because Jerusalem had already begun to figure in Disraeli's fantasies as a future Jewish metropolis that he spent so little time describing its fallen actuality. He did not visit the Jewish quarter, apparently, and the sights that he dwelled on in his novels were not Jewish ones but the Church of the Holy Sepulchre and especially the Dome of the Rock ("a glorious glimpse of splendid courts, and light airy gates of Saracenic triumph"). Not until later, when he transformed his actual experiences in Jerusalem into the Jewish fantasies of *Alroy* and *Tancred*, did the true importance of Disraeli's time in Palestine become clear.

After Palestine, Disraeli spent several months exploring

Egypt. Originally he planned to stay abroad even longer, making his way back north through Italy. But in July 1831, while he was in Cairo, his companion Meredith died suddenly of smallpox, and he decided to return home immediately to comfort his bereft sister. Writing Sarah with the tragic news, Disraeli vowed to make up for the fiancé she had lost: "Live then, my heart's treasure, for one who has ever loved you with a surpassing love. . . . Be my genius, my solace, my companion, my joy." Today this sounds like a strange way for a brother to comfort a sister, if only because of its apparent egotism. But it would not necessarily have sounded that way to Sarah, who at the age of twenty-eight was facing a long future as a spinster.

In fact, Disraeli was offering her exactly the gift that he gave to a series of women over the years: the chance to participate, if only vicariously, in the public, political world that was otherwise closed to them. To be the "genius" and "companion" of a rising politician was a kind of career for Sarah, and provided much of the pleasure of her life for the next thirty years. Of course, the arrangement also suited Disraeli perfectly; for by the time he arrived home in October, he had decided on a plan that would require all of Sarah's practical and moral support. Finally, after years of dreaming about it, Disraeli was determined to get into Parliament.

6

Disraeli returned to a country in the midst of a constitutional crisis. In the year and a half since he left England, the issue of parliamentary reform, long simmering on the back burner of British politics, had finally boiled over. The revolution of 1830 in France, which replaced the old Bourbon dynasty with a constitutional monarchy, fed the hopes of reformers in Britain, and showed the establishment what might be in store if change was not forthcoming. In November, the first Whig government in half a century came to power under Lord Grey, with a mandate to pass a Reform Bill that would quiet the country once and for all.

Disraeli followed the ensuing struggle during his travels, whenever he could get news from home or find an English-language newspaper. In March 1831, the House of Commons passed a Reform Bill by one vote, but it was soon killed in committee. The Whigs then called a general election, which returned a larger pro-Reform majority in the Commons. But in October, the House of Lords rejected the Bill a second time, whereupon protests and riots broke out around the country. The obstinacy of the landed gentry and the Tory Party, which remained strong in the upper house, seemed about to push Britain over the brink of revolution. Not until the king, the newly crowned William IV, promised to create as many new peers as it took to secure the Bill's passage did the House of Lords relent. In June 1832, the Reform Bill finally became law.

Today, when universal suffrage is taken for granted in any free society, the effects of the Reform Bill look modest enough. Under the old franchise, out of a population of sixteen and a half million, about five hundred thousand men in Britain had the right to vote. By lowering the property qualifications for voters, the Bill enfranchised some three hundred thousand new voters, mainly urban and middle-class. Equally important, the Bill abolished dozens of rotten boroughs, transferring their seats to the new industrial cities of the north. But corruption was still endemic; the new electorate was still just one-seventh of the adult male population; and no one even considered giving the vote to women.

Symbolically, however, the Reform Bill amounted to a revolution, and supporters and opponents alike received it as one. For the first time since 1688, when the Glorious Revolution established the principle that Parliament, not the king, held supreme power, Britain took a decisive step toward greater democracy. A principle had been enshrined, and the reforming impulse would dominate British politics for the next half-century. The men at the top of the political pyramid were still mainly aristocrats—of the ten prime ministers who followed Grey, seven had titles—but the middle class now had a voice in Parliament, and an increasingly dominant one. The great legislative achievements of the mid-Victorian period would be to modernize, liberalize, and rationalize the institutions of the country. Law, education, the colonies, the army, the Church: one by one, over the next fifty years, they would all be reformed.

In almost every case, the impetus for reform would come from the Whigs and their successors, the Liberals. The Liberal monopoly on reform helps to explain why, in the forty years after the passage of the Reform Bill, the Tories were in office for just ten. Already in 1832, as Disraeli laid the groundwork for his first campaign, it was clear that the Whigs were going to be in charge for a long time to come. Yet Disraeli, who wanted nothing more than power, declared himself from the very start of his career an enemy of the party in power. As he said in one of his early speeches: "Gentlemen, had I been a political adventurer, I had nothing to do but to join the Whigs; but conscientiously believing that their policy was in every way pernicious, I felt it my duty to oppose them."

But in the summer of 1832, as Disraeli planned to run for Parliament in High Wycombe, his father's borough, he was not sure that he wanted to be a Tory, either. By defying Reform, the Tories had made themselves seem antiquated and unelectable, and it was certain that the first election on the reformed franchise would produce a Whig landslide. So Disraeli decided to try his luck without any party support, hoping that the unpredictable currents of the Reform tidal wave would carry him to victory. "I start in the high Radical interest," he wrote. "Toryism is worn out & I cannot condescend to be a Whig." It was, to say the least, a strange start for a politician who would become a Conservative icon. And like so many of the impetuous decisions of his early years, it was to cost him dearly later on. The fact that Disraeli started his career as a "high Radical" branded him as unreliable, even unprincipled, long after he had become a stalwart of the Tory Party.

In truth, what Disraeli was really banking on, more than his party affiliation or his stand on the issues, was the sheer force of his character. Despite his early setbacks, he had not lost Vivian Grey's sense of being destined for greatness. He was in love with politics long before he had anything like a political philosophy, and he always believed in himself more than in any platform. He practically said as much in an election pamphlet published in 1833, under the egotistical title *What Is He?:* "Let us not forget also an influence too much underrated in this age of bustling mediocrity—the influence of individual character. Great spirits may yet arise to guide the groaning helm through the world of troubled waters—spirits whose proud destiny it may still be at the same time to maintain the glory of the Empire, and to secure the happiness of the People."

The electors of High Wycombe, it turned out, were not interested in having a great spirit represent them in Parliament. Disraeli first campaigned there in June 1832, when the resignation of one of the sitting MPs prompted a by-election. The Reform Bill had just been passed, and Disraeli was already intending to run in the general election planned for December on the new franchise. But he couldn't pass up the chance to contest the empty seat, hoping that the borough's Tories and Radicals would vote for him to keep the Whigs out. He made a valiant effort, including a storied speech in front of the town's Red Lion Inn. "When the poll is declared I shall be there," he said, pointing to the head of the lion, "and my opponent will be there," pointing to the tail.

Disraeli's opponent, however, was Charles Grey, the son of the prime minister, and the famous name proved impossible to beat. Grey received twenty votes to Disraeli's twelve—figures that suggest the tiny scale of the pre-Reform electorate in some boroughs. When the same candidates returned for the general election in December, this time on the expanded franchise, Disraeli again shunned party labels, deriding the "factious slang of Whig and Tory—two names with one meaning"; and again Grey beat him, this time by 140 votes to 119.

Losing two elections in the space of six months was the kind of humiliation that once might have sent Disraeli into a deep depression. But at twenty-eight, he was already a different man than he had been at twenty-one. Never again would a setback—and there were many still to come—cause him to lose faith in himself. A few weeks later, he was in the gallery of the House of Commons, listening to the speeches of what he was certain would be his future colleagues. "Between ourselves," he confided in a letter to his sister, "I could floor them all. This *entre nous:* I was never more confident of anything than that I could carry everything before me in that House. The time will come."

He proved his determination by declaring himself a candidate yet again, for a seat in Marylebone that was expected to become vacant early in 1833. As it turned out, no election took place, but Disraeli's persistence was beginning to make his name known in wider political circles. It was around this time that a newspaper ran a satirical squib about him, which he quoted in a letter to Sarah: "some one asked Disraeli, in offering himself for Marylebone, on what he intended *to stand*. 'On my head,' was the reply."

Disraeli offers no comment, but he must have been delighted. The joke captured his insouciant humor, which was to mark him out from the general run of English politicians for the rest of his life. ("An insular country subject to fogs, and with a powerful middle class, requires grave statesmen," he teased in his last novel.) But Disraeli was also standing "on his head" in a more serious sense. Most candidates for Parliament relied on their family names and their local connections. As a Jew, Disraeli had neither of these strong supports. All he could put in their place was his intelligence, and the will to use it. It was inevitable that some wit came up with the nickname "the Jew d'esprit."

Even as a child, however, Disraeli had recognized that it would not be enough to impress the English with his head. He would also have to prove that his heart was in the right place, that his loyalty to England was unimpeachable. It is no wonder, then, that as Disraeli evolved his distinctive political philosophy, in a series of articles, pamphlets, and speeches, the idea of the nation came to the forefront. Already in the 1830s, he found the formula that was to guide his political career. While the Whigs were the party of a selfish class, he argued, the Tories were the party of the whole nation. They were the defenders not just of England's traditional institutions, including the nobility and the Church, but also of the workers and farmers those institutions were obligated to serve. Once he reached this conclusion, Disraeli had no hesitation about officially joining the Conservative Party. Both his aristocratic self-image and his need to demonstrate his loyalty dictated that Disraeli join the party of what he called "the gentlemen of England."

The decision was made easier by the fact that, as an Independent, his political career was going nowhere. At the end of 1834 there was a new election at High Wycombe. For a third time Disraeli threw his hat in the ring, and once again he lost to Charles Grey. Immediately after, he wrote to the Duke of Wellington, the Conservative leader, offering his allegiance. In fact, he had already begun the difficult task of publicly reconciling his Radical past with his Tory future.

To most people, the two labels seemed diametrically opposed; a Tory Radical made no more sense than a Republican Socialist would in American politics today. Disraeli argued, however, that what Tories and Radicals had in common was a vision of an organic nation. The Tories traditionally identified the nation with its ruling class and its ancient institutions, while the Radicals thought England belonged to the whole people, including workers and the poor. Now that the Reform Bill had begun to democratize political power, however, the Tories had no choice but to broaden their conception of the nation. To survive as a political force, they had to show that the landed gentry could be trusted to look beyond their class interest and genuinely serve the public interest. "If the Tories indeed despair of restoring the aristocratic principle," Disraeli wrote, "it is their duty to coalesce with the Radicals, and permit both political nicknames to merge in the common, the intelligible, and the dignified title of a National Party."

Such a merger would give the Tories a moral and political advantage over the Whigs, whom Disraeli considered "not a national party, influenced by any great and avowed principles of public policy and conduct, but a small knot of great families who have no other object but their own aggrandisement, and who seek to gratify it by all possible means." In his rough polemics against the Whigs (in one article he referred to the attorney general, a Scot, as "this booing, fawning, jobbing progeny of haggis and cockaleekie"), Disraeli continually returned to the charge that they were responsible for perverting English traditions with foreign ideas. In 1688, by replacing the legitimate King James II with the more amenable William III, the Whig nobles imposed a "Venetian constitution" on England, turning a once powerful monarch into an enfeebled doge. At the same time, by encouraging deficit spending, they condemned England to "Dutch finance." With this sort of rhetorical jujitsu, Disraeli turned the venerable Whig aristocrats into foreigners, while leaving himself, a Jew, as the true vindicator of Britannia's honor. (His most extensive work of political theory was titled *Vindication of the English Constitution*.)

Disraeli's definition of Toryism was too original to be very popular, but it did succeed in establishing him, by the middle of the decade, as one of the party's up-and-coming men. In 1835, when he went to Taunton to run for Parliament a fourth time, it was as the official Tory candidate. On the platform, one observer wrote, he was equally striking for his foppish clothes and his "physiognomy," which was "strictly Jewish": "Never in my life had I been so struck by a face as I was by that of Disraeli. It was lividly pale, and from beneath two finely-arched eyebrows blazed out a pair of intensely black eyes. I have never seen such orbs in mortal sockets, either before or since."

Disraeli was not striking enough, however, or perhaps he was a little too striking. For the fourth time, he was defeated. But the most significant result of the election was still to come. In one campaign speech, Disraeli attacked the Whigs for making a political alliance with Daniel O'Connell, the Irish Catholic leader, "whom they had denounced as a traitor" in the past. Newspaper reports, however, made it sound as if Disraeli himself had called O'Connell a traitor; and O'Connell, whose endorsement Disraeli had solicited back in his Radical days, was furious. He responded with a speech in Dublin, in which he called Disraeli, among other things, a "reptile," and accused him of "perfidy, selfishness, depravity, and want of principle." The supreme insult, however, came at the end, when O'Connell declaimed:

> His name shows that he is of Jewish origin. I do not use it as a term of reproach; there are many most respectable Jews. But there are, as in every other people, some of the lowest and most disgusting grade of moral turpitude; and of those I look upon Mr. Disraeli as the worst. He has just the qualities of the impenitent thief on the Cross, and I verily believe, if Mr. Disraeli's family herald were to be examined and his genealogy traced, the same personage would be discovered to be the heir at law of the exalted individual to whom I allude.

O'Connell was not, it is only fair to acknowledge, a confirmed anti-Semite. During the debate over Jewish emancipation, he boasted that Ireland "is the only Christian country that I know of unsullied by any one act of persecution of the Jews," and took the position that the rights he had won for Catholics should be shared equally by Jews. In his rage against Disraeli, however, he resorted to anti-Semitism of an especially poisonous kind. Disraeli was no stranger to Jew-baiting, and he schooled himself to ignore it most of the time. In 1841, when he was running for reelection to Parliament, he was undaunted when hecklers waved pieces of pork in his face, or when a man drove up on a donkey shouting, "I come here to take you back to Jerusalem."

But O'Connell's remarks represented a crucial test for

Disraeli, as he immediately recognized. Most of the time, the anti-Semitism directed against him was essentially snobbish, a way of bringing up his "low" origins, or xenophobic, playing on popular hostility to "foreigners." O'Connell's remarks were more dangerous because they evoked ancient, theological anti-Semitism, in particular the charge of deicide. If such language became widely acceptable—if even being a Christian did not prevent people from thinking of him as a Christ-killer—Disraeli's political career would be doomed.

His response, then, was swift and extremely strong. Not only did he publish an open letter, pointing out the irony of O'Connell, the defender of the Catholics, appealing to religious prejudice: "I see that you are quite prepared to persecute." He also wanted to challenge him to a duel; but since O'Connell, who once killed a man in a duel, had vowed publicly never to fight again, Disraeli instead sent a challenge to his son. When the son refused, Disraeli tried to goad him into combat, promising to "take every opportunity of holding your father's name up to public contempt." Finally the police got involved, and Disraeli was compelled to post a bond for his good conduct.

This sort of scandal was not, one might think, the best thing that could happen to a novice politician of uncertain reputation. Yet Disraeli was sincerely delighted with the way the O'Connell affair turned out. "There is but one opinion among *all* parties," he wrote boisterously to Sarah, "viz., that I have *squabashed* them." By turning a political controversy into an affair of honor, Disraeli effectively neutralized O'Connell's attack: he showed the world that he was as jealous of his honor as any gentleman, and thus bore no resemblance to "the impenitent thief on the Cross." And his eagerness to fight a duel advertised his physical bravery, an essential virtue in a society still guided by aristocratic codes of manliness. The Tories may not have liked to be reminded that Disraeli was a Jew, but they had to admit that he was not a coward.

7

While Disraeli's political career inched forward, his literary career was flourishing. He had returned from his Eastern tour with the ideas for his next two novels well advanced. Writing with his usual speed, he managed to publish *Contarini Fleming* in 1832, a month before his first run for Parliament, and *Alroy* less than a year later. Neither book sold as well as *Vivian Grey*, but they were more serious than anything Disraeli had written so far. *Contarini* in particular, whose subtitle—*A Psychological Romance*—suggests its high ambition, won the admiration of judges like Mary Shelley and William Beckford.

To Disraeli, his novels taken together constituted a self-portrait. "My works are the embodification of my feelings," he wrote. "In *Vivian Grey* I have portrayed my active and real ambition; in *Alroy* my ideal ambition; *The Psychological Romance* is a development of my poetic character. This trilogy is the secret history of my feelings—I shall write no more about myself." The insistent focus on his own ambition and character accounts for the limitations of the novels—none of them are great works of fiction, and today they are mainly read for insights into the mind of their author. But it also explains why writing the novels was so important to

Disraeli's development. He had learned early on—as early as his first reading of Shakespeare—that the English imagination of Jews was as restrictive as English laws about Jews were tolerant. The first step toward realizing his ambitions was necessarily to escape those restrictions—to cancel the sordid English stereotypes about Jews by asserting the exuberance, idealism, and pride that were the truths of his own experience. Indirectly in *Contarini Fleming* and explicitly in *Alroy*, Disraeli reclaimed the imaginative freedom to define Jewishness, and himself as a Jew, on his own terms. In this sense, it was necessary for Disraeli to be a novelist before he could be a statesman, and his career as a statesman was a continuation of the work of self-invention that he began as a novelist.

Contarini Fleming was Disraeli's favorite of his own novels, perhaps because it was the first one with which he had taken real pains. "I shall always consider *The Psychological* as the perfection of English prose and a chef d'oeuvre," he wrote, only half-joking. No reader today would agree, and the fact that Disraeli was so impressed with the book is perhaps the clearest proof that he was not a born novelist. As in *Vivian Grey*, he obviously ran out of ideas long before he ran out of space, and he was forced to eke out the last third of the book with long quotations from the letters he had written home from the East. Perhaps if Disraeli had undergone the discipline of writing for serial publication, like most of the great Victorian novelists, he would have learned better how to sustain a plot and hold the reader's interest. Instead, he wrote his novels in a single sprint, and his pace usually faltered toward the end.

Still, if *Contarini Fleming* is not a great novel, it is a vitally important document of Disraeli's mind. Indeed, it is a classic bildungsroman, in which a sensitive young man discovers that he does not fit into ordinary society because he is a genius. Contarini Fleming, the narrator, displays all the hallmarks of the type. He dismays his family with bouts of temper, he gets into fights at school, he falls poetically in love with a series of women. Yet because Contarini's creator is not quite an artist, he cannot find a happy ending, like most such heroes, by discovering his own artistic calling. He does have a momentary epiphany: " 'Am I, then,' I exclaimed, looking around with an astonished and vacant air, 'Am I, then, after all, a poet?' " But Disraeli's heart is not really in it, and the scenes in which Contarini rhapsodizes like a poet are the least convincing in the book.

We seem to hear the author's voice, rather, when Contarini's father tells him that it is better to be a man of action than a man of letters: "We are active beings, and our sympathy, above all other sympathies, is with great action." Fortunately, Mr. Fleming happens to be the prime minister of a small Scandinavian country and is able to give his son high government office. This allows Disraeli to plunge once again into his favorite imaginative game, playing at politics; and Contarini, more successful than Vivian Grey, pulls off a major diplomatic coup. Disraeli conjures his political exultation far more convincingly than his poetic inspiration:

"There seemed to me no achievement of which I was not capable, and of which I was not ambitious. In imagination I shook thrones and founded empires." On the evidence of *Contarini Fleming*, Disraeli could never consider literature more than a temporary substitute for politics.

Yet even political success does not bring Contarini happiness. For he has always felt, even as a child, that he is essentially different from the Scandinavians who surround him. Contarini's father is "a Saxon nobleman of ancient family," but his dead mother was Italian—dark, exotic, passionate. As a result, even Contarini's half-brothers seem to him to belong to a different species: "They were called my brothers, but Nature gave the lie to the reiterated assertion. There was no similitude between us. Their blue eyes, their flaxen hair, and their white visages claimed no kindred with my Venetian countenance. Wherever I moved I looked around me, and beheld a race different from myself. . . . I knew not why, but I was unhappy."

Contarini may not know why, but it is obvious to the reader that Disraeli has found a way to give his hero a fictional equivalent of his own Jewishness. Contarini, too, is a child of the Mediterranean marooned in a Northern country. "There was no sympathy," he complains, "between my frame and the rigid clime whither I had been brought to live." As a young man, however, Contarini makes a saving discovery, the same one Disraeli made during his travels in Spain and Palestine: he may be a misfit in the North, but in the South he is a prince. Reading a history of Venice, Contarini happens across his own first name: "But when I read that there were yet four families of such pre-eminent ancestry that they were placed even above the magnificoes, being reputed descendants of Roman Consular houses, and that of these the unrivalled race of Contarini was the chief, I dashed down the book in a paroxysm of nervous exultation, and rushed into the woods."

In Contarini's reclaiming of his Venetian name, Disraeli offers a moving symbol of his own newfound attitude toward Jewishness: at last he has found a way to turn his alienation into a source of pride. It is Disraeli's version of the great Romantic fable of the Ugly Duckling (Hans Christian Andersen, in fact, was nearly his exact contemporary). But in keeping with Disraeli's constant preoccupations as a Jew and an aspiring politician, he gives the story an ethnic and political coloring. It is the historical grandeur of Venice and his Venetian ancestors that emboldens Contarini to succeed in politics and poetry. Eventually he makes a pilgrimage to Venice, and like Disraeli at the Alhambra, he finds that he is the heir to kings: "The marble palaces of my ancestors rose on each side, like a series of vast and solemn temples. . . . How willingly would I have given my life to have once more filled their mighty halls with the proud retainers of their free and victorious nobles!" At the novel's end, after many romantic travails, Contarini is still dreaming of a return to politics, this time as his people's savior: "Perchance also the political regeneration of the country to which I am devoted may not be distant, and in that great work I am resolved to participate."

When Disraeli wrote these words, the revolution of 1848,

which saw Venice briefly liberated from the Austrians, was still sixteen years in the future. (The leader of the Venetian Republic, Daniele Manin, was a Jew—a fact that Disraeli noted with pride, perhaps seeing in him an alter ego like Contarini.) But while Disraeli believed, or at least claimed to believe, that his own ancestors once lived in Venice, his Eastern tour had already turned his thoughts to the country that was the Jewish people's original homeland, Palestine. And in 1833, the notion of a "political regeneration" of the Jewish people in Palestine seemed impossibly remote. Yet Disraeli's Romantic imagination, his personal longing for glory, and his largely mythical understanding of Jewish history combined to give him a visionary understanding of the possibilities of Zionism, long before his more realistic contemporaries. More than sixty years before Theodor Herzl's *The Jewish State*, almost thirty years before Moses Hess's *Rome and Jerusalem*, Disraeli was already dreaming about a Jewish homeland in Palestine.

In *The Wondrous Tale of Alroy*, he would bring that dream into the open, for the first time in modern literature. In a preface to a later edition of the novel, Disraeli wrote that he had been "attracted" to the "marvellous career" of David Alroy even as a child. But Disraeli's Alroy bears little resemblance to the minor figure mentioned by Benjamin of Tudela, the Spanish Jew whose *Travels* are a classic of medieval Hebrew literature. According to Benjamin, Alroy, a Kurdish Jew, raised a revolt against the Seljuk Turks in Azerbaijan around 1160. He was credited with magic powers by his followers, who proclaimed him the Messiah; but this pretension won him the hostility of Jewish leaders in Baghdad, who begged him not to antagonize the Turks. Finally he was betrayed by his father-in-law and killed, probably without winning a single battle.

Disraeli's Alroy is a much grander figure, a kind of Jewish Alexander the Great. In his novel, Alroy wins victory after victory, conquers Baghdad, and comes close to establishing a new empire in the Middle East. There is also a good deal of what Disraeli called "supernatural machinery" in the novel, including a magic ring, a secret underground temple, and the Scepter of Solomon, which Alroy must claim if he is to conquer Jerusalem. Disraeli writes that all this is based on Jewish tradition—"Cabalistical and correct," as he puts it—but it is clear that the real sources of the novel's mysticism lie in *The Thousand and One Nights*, the Eastern tales of Byron, and the quest poems of Shelley. In general, *Alroy* is better understood as high Orientalist fantasy than historical fiction. Even Disraeli's prose, whose emphatic rhythms and repetitions suggest that some sections started out as verse, is kitschily intoxicated: " 'Ah! bright gazelle! Ah! bright gazelle!' the princess cried, the princess cried; 'thy lips are softer than the swan, thy lips are softer than the swan; but his breathed passion when they pressed, my bright gazelle! my bright gazelle!' "

But if *Alroy* seems impossibly overripe today, its psychological core remains entirely serious. Disraeli said that he began to write the novel in Jerusalem in 1831, at a moment when he was pondering the role Jewishness might play in his own life and career. And in his hands, the story of David Alroy becomes a veiled meditation on the state of the Jews in Europe, and a parable of his own possible future.

From the beginning of the novel, Alroy, a descendant of King David, rages against the degradation of the Jews under Muslim rule. Yet as Disraeli makes clear, the condition of the Jews is hardly unbearable. On the contrary, Alroy's uncle, Bostenay, is a rich man, and enjoys the honorary title of Prince of the Captivity. "The age of power has passed; it is by prudence now that we must flourish," he declares. He is, perhaps, Disraeli's critical portrait of the wealthy English Jews of his own day, who had all the advantages of wealth but none of the dignity of power.

Alroy, like Disraeli himself, cannot be satisfied with making money. He is disgusted by the state to which his people have fallen: "I am ashamed, uncle, ashamed, ashamed," he tells Bostenay. The action begins when, in an episode borrowed from the story of Moses, Alroy sees a Turkish official accost his sister and impetuously kills him. He is forced to flee into the desert and is about to die of thirst when he is rescued by Jabaster, a magician and fanatical Jewish patriot. When Alroy has a dream of being acclaimed by a vast army as "the great Messiah of our ancient hopes," Jabaster decides that the young man represents his long-awaited chance to reestablish the kingdom of David. After a series of adventures, Alroy begins to put Jabaster's plan into action, scattering the Turks and conquering Baghdad.

But in the meantime, Alroy has acquired another advisor—Jabaster's brother and mirror image, Honain. Honain represents the tempting path of what Isaac called "amalgamation": he has achieved wealth and honor, but only at the price of "passing" as a Muslim. In his own view, however, he has not betrayed his people, but simply effected his own liberation. "I too would be free and honoured," he tells Alroy in a resonant phrase; "Freedom and honour are mine, but I was my own messiah." Honain introduces Alroy to the beautiful Princess Schirene, the daughter of the caliph, and though she is a Muslim he falls in love with her. ("The daughters of my tribe, they please me not, though they are passing fair," Alroy admits—a sentiment Disraeli shared.)

But now, at the height of his fortune, with an empire in his grasp and a princess for his wife, Alroy begins to succumb to Honain's worldly counsel. Why, he asks, should he abandon wealthy, cosmopolitan Baghdad, in order to set up his capital in the small, graceless city of Jerusalem? Why should it not be his destiny to rule over an empire of all the nations of the East, rather than become the Messiah of the Jews alone? "The world is mine: and shall I yield the prize, the universal and heroic prize, to realise the dull tradition of some dreaming priest, and consecrate a legend?" Alroy asks. "Is the Lord of Hosts so slight a God, that we must place a barrier to His sovereignty, and fix the boundaries of Omnipotence between the Jordan and the Lebanon?" Mischievously, Disraeli even makes Alroy speak in the stock phrases of modern English liberalism: "Universal empire must not be founded on sectarian prejudices and exclusive rights."

Jabaster tries to recall his king to the righteous Jewish

path, but to no avail. At last he attempts a coup against Alroy, but he is defeated and sentenced to death. From that moment, however, God's favor deserts Alroy. In his next battle he is defeated, and a Muslim king, Alp Arslan, takes him prisoner. Now Honain reappears with one last temptation: if Alroy converts to Islam, his life will be spared. But the scion of the house of David has learned his lesson. His strength is not his own but his nation's, and individual glory means nothing next to the redemption of the Jews. He taunts Alp Arslan with his refusal, and the king, in a rage, cuts off his head.

For Disraeli, writing at the beginning of his own career as an English politician, the moral of *Alroy* was deeply ambiguous. With typical immodesty, he imagines the paths open to him as a choice between messiahships. To become a Jewish national leader, like Alroy, would mean trying to fulfill the messianic hope of restoring the Jews to the Promised Land. Indeed, the redemption of Israel was a potent strain, not just in Jewish liturgy, with which Disraeli was not very familiar, but also in English literature and culture, where he could not have avoided encountering it. Ever since Cromwell readmitted the Jews to England, actuated by the hope that "God will bring the Jews home to their station from the isles of the sea" (as he told Parliament in 1653), certain English Protestants had looked forward to the restoration of the Jews to the Promised Land.

Around the time of the Damascus Affair, in fact, an influential lobby of evangelical Christians urged Lord Palmerston, the foreign minister, to commit Britain to the creation of a Jewish home in Palestine. Their goals were partly pragmatic—as the Jews' official protector, Britain would gain a voice in the affairs of the Ottoman Empire, such as Russia enjoyed as the protector of Turkey's Orthodox Christians. "There are two parties here," wrote the British consul in Jerusalem in 1839, "who will doubtless have some voice in the future disposition of affairs. The one is the Jew—unto whom God originally gave this land for a possession, and the other, the Protestant Christian, his legitimate offspring. Of both these Great Britain seems the natural guardian."

The suggestion that Protestant Britain was the direct heir to Israel, and peculiarly responsible for the Jews' fate, also carried a strong millenarian charge. Lord Shaftesbury, a pious peer who was for many decades president of the Society for Promoting Christianity Among the Jews, told Palmerston that bringing back the Jews to Zion would be a way of hastening the end times. "Anxious about the hopes and prospects of the Jewish people," he wrote in his diary in 1840. "Everything seems ripe for their return to Palestine; 'the way of the kings of the East is prepared,' " he observed, quoting the Book of Revelation.

In the end nothing came of this enthusiasm, which took account neither of diplomatic realities in the Middle East, nor of the needs and desires of actual Jews. It was, rather, another manifestation of the old English habit of preferring imaginary Jews to real ones, condemning Judaism to play a role in a Christian drama. So strong was the identification of

English hopes with Jewish hopes that William Blake could actually fuse the two in his famous poem "Jerusalem": "I will not cease from mental fight,/Nor shall my sword sleep in my hand,/Till we have built Jerusalem/In England's green and pleasant Land." For Disraeli, always alert to both Jewish and English aspirations, the idea that he might be the one to build Jerusalem—to restore Jewish dignity while fulfilling Christian prophecy—was just adequate to his dreams of his world-historical destiny.

Yet *Alroy* also offers another vision of deliverance: the self-liberation that Honain boasts of when he says, "I was my own messiah." This was the emancipated Jew's alternative to Alroy's antique hope—the idea that the only liberation a Jew really needs is liberation from Judaism, with all its outmoded taboos and social disadvantages. And for a Jew in Disraeli's position—already baptized as a Christian, already making his way in gentile society—this sort of self-deliverance seemed infinitely more practical than Alroy's grand schemes. Indeed, even Alroy is tempted to escape from his limiting Jewish context in order to become the cosmopolitan leader his gifts qualify him to be. Disraeli's novel has a moral seriousness that one would not suspect from its gaudy surface, because it poses a quintessential Jewish dilemma in bold terms. Does Alroy—which is to say, does Disraeli—owe his gifts to the Jewish people, or to himself and the world?

In light of Disraeli's later career, the answer *Alroy* offers to this question is deeply ironic. The novel does not endorse the Jewish sectarianism of Jabaster—Disraeli echoes his father's hatred of priestcraft—but it clearly repudiates the plausible assimilationism of Honain, which leads only to dishonor and disaster. Indeed, it is Disraeli's distinction between Jewish belief and Jewish solidarity, and his insistence that it is possible to have the latter without the former, that makes *Alroy* a significant proto-Zionist text. Disraeli anticipates Moses Hess's argument that "the pious Jew is above all a Jewish patriot." If he had obeyed the novel's logic in his own life, if he had tried to translate Alroy's vision to the nineteenth century, Disraeli might have become a real-life Daniel Deronda.

But *Alroy* was a fantasy, not a program, and by the time he published it, Disraeli had already decided that he would be his own messiah—that England, not Israel, would be the Israel of his imagination. Writing *Alroy* served Disraeli, it seems, as a a kind of exorcism. By imagining a fantastic alternative career for himself as a Jewish political leader, he convinced himself that that career was impossible. And, in fact, there is no way that Disraeli, in the 1830s, could have played the role that Herzl played in the 1890s. It was not until after Disraeli's death that the rise of political anti-Semitism, and the increasing persecution of Jews in Russia, made the necessity of Zionism clear to the Jews themselves; and it was not until Zionism became necessary that it could appear credible. In the Europe Disraeli knew, the proto-Zionism of *Alroy* could only be an "ideal ambition." For his "active and real ambition," we have to look to the less glorious figure of Vivian Grey.

Disraeli may have followed the advice Honain gives to

Alroy: "With your person and talents you may be grand vizir. Clear your head of nonsense." But in some part of his mind, he always kept faith with Alroy's national "nonsense." The diaries of Lord Stanley offer a surprising confirmation of this. In the 1850s, when Stanley was serving his apprenticeship in politics, he was more than a little fascinated by the exotic figure of Disraeli. In his journals, he is continually trying to figure out whether Disraeli was ever in earnest—whether he had political principles, or merely political tactics. "There is certainly a very prevalent impression," he writes, "that Disraeli has no well-defined opinions of his own: but is content to adopt, and defend, any which may be popular with the Conservative party at the time."

There is just one moment in the diaries when Stanley believes he is seeing Disraeli genuinely inspired. It comes during a visit Stanley paid Disraeli at the beginning of 1851, twenty years after he visited Palestine:

On one occasion, during this very visit, he talked to me with great apparent earnestness on the subject of restoring the Jews to their own land. . . . The country, he said, had ample natural capabilities; all it wanted was labour, and protection for the labourer: the ownership of the soil might be bought from Turkey: money would be forthcoming: the Rothschilds and leading Hebrew capitalists would all help: the Turkish empire was falling into ruin: the Turkish Govt would do anything for money: all that was necessary was to establish colonies, with rights over the soil, and security from ill treatment. The question of nationality might wait until these had taken hold. He added that these ideas were extensively entertained among the nation. A man who should carry them out would be the next Messiah, the true Saviour of his people.

It is almost exactly the program Herzl would advance in *The Jewish State* in 1896. Who can say, after all, what might have happened if Disraeli, who knew so many English and European statesmen, had advanced it half a century earlier? Yet by the time Disraeli revealed this buried part of his mind to Stanley, he had long since realized that being prime minister of England and being "the next Messiah" were incompatible goals. Indeed, Stanley writes, "he never recurred to it again," and in later years, "I have heard of no practical step taken, or attempted to be taken, by him in the matter." Stanley was left to wonder whether "the whole scene was a mystification. . . . But which purpose could the mystification, if it were one, serve?" The answer, as *Alroy* shows, is that it was not a mystification; it was another life, which Disraeli was destined never to lead.

8

While Disraeli chased every available opportunity to get into Parliament, he was not idle in between elections. His literary reputation and his exotic good looks made him welcome in the salons of London, where he mixed with men of fashion, titled ladies, and Tory politicians. He detailed his social conquests in letters to Sarah: "I have had great success in society this year," he bragged in 1834. "I am as popular with the dandies as I was hated by the second-rate men. I make my way easily in the highest set, where there is no envy, malice, &c., and where they like to admire and be amused." In an age when the worlds of politics and high society overlapped, the ability to amuse and be amused opened important doors for Disraeli.

Just how completely his personal life dovetailed with his political career can be seen in his relations with Henrietta Sykes, whom he met in 1833. Henrietta was the perfect woman for Disraeli at this stage of his life. Older, married, and well connected, she was able to help his career without demanding a commitment in return. The two of them fell passionately, theatrically in love, with the connivance of Henrietta's husband (who was himself sleeping with Clara Bolton, Disraeli's former mistress). As in all of Disraeli's most successful relationships with women, there was a strong maternal element in the affair. One passionate letter from Henrietta ends, "I would be such an affectionate old Nurse to my child and kiss and soothe every pain. . . . Sleep and dream of—your Mother." Yet it was also an unambiguously sexual relationship, as other letters of Henrietta's leave no doubt: in one she refers to "ten happy minutes on the sopha," and in another she seems to worry that she might be pregnant ("Do you think any misery can occur to us *now* from all the loved embraces?").

Disraeli's affair with Henrietta lasted three years and furnished him with the inspiration for his next novel—as well as the heroine's name. *Henrietta Temple*, an effusive but conventional love story, was a commercial success in 1836, though it holds little interest for the reader today. Disraeli's rhapsodies on the power of love must have been inspired by his feelings for Henrietta, but they come across on the page as willed and hyperbolic. It is very characteristic of Disraeli to praise true love by declaring that it can even supersede his greatest passion, ambition. "To feel our flaunty ambition fade away like a shrivelled gourd before her vision; to feel fame a juggle and posterity a lie; and to be prepared at once, for this great object, to forfeit and fling away all former hopes, ties, schemes, views . . . this is a lover, and this is love!"

In reality, however, Disraeli's affair with Henrietta Sykes was closely connected with his ambition. It was at Henrietta's house that he first met Lord Lyndhurst, a Tory elder statesman who was also a famous ladies' man. According to a durable rumor, Disraeli more or less traded his mistress to Lyndhurst in exchange for political favors. Things may not have been so sordidly straightforward, but it is certain that by the time his affair with Henrietta ended, Disraeli was well established as Lyndhurst's protégé. His next novel, *Venetia*—a roman à clef loosely based on the lives of Byron and Shelley—was dedicated to Lyndhurst.

Venetia was an interesting departure for Disraeli, the first of his novels that does not read like an exercise in self-projection or wish fulfillment. If he had continued as a professional novelist, it might have marked the beginning of a new, more objective kind of storytelling. But Disraeli wrote *Venetia* far too rapidly to take pains with it. By 1837, he was in such straits that he had to write as fast as he could, simply to earn enough to put off his creditors a little longer. His debts, which had once been a stimulant, were starting to become a serious threat to his political career. The scandal of an arrest, he knew, would wreck his reputation. In December 1836, when he was invited to give the keynote speech at a Conservative Party banquet, he begged his lawyer to keep the bailiffs from finding out: "I have been requested to move the principal toast 'The House of Lords.' I trust there is no danger of my being nabbed, as this would be a fatal *contretemps*, inasmuch as, in all probability, I am addressing my future constituents."

Getting into Parliament, then, had become a race against the clock. If he were "nabbed" before he could find a seat, he would be ruined; once he became an MP, however, he would enjoy immunity from arrest. Finally, in the summer of 1837, the death of King William IV gave Disraeli his chance. The accession of the new monarch, Queen Victoria, meant that a general election would be called, and Disraeli now stood high enough in the Tory ranks to be offered a winnable seat. The Carlton Club, which served as party headquarters, sent him down to the borough of Maidstone, which already had one Conservative MP, Wyndham Lewis, and seemed ready to elect another. His running mate's wealth was a major advantage for Disraeli: getting into Parliament meant spending a small fortune in bribes, and Lewis was willing to foot the bill. It didn't hurt that Lewis's wife, Mary Anne, whom Disraeli had met at parties in London, boosted him strongly. "Mark what I prophesy," she wrote. "Mr. Disraeli will in a very few years be one of the greatest men of his day." Neither of them suspected yet just how large a role Mary Anne would play in making that prophecy come true.

The Maidstone contest was Disraeli's fifth campaign, and by now he was immune to the gross and subtle varieties of Jew-baiting that greeted him. When troublemakers in the crowd disrupted his speeches with shouts of "Shylock," he ignored them; and when a supporter of his Radical opponent drew attention to Disraeli's Jewish name, he was ready with a comeback. "Mr. Disraeli—I hope I pronounce his name right," the speaker said; at a stump speech the next day, Disraeli pretended to have the same difficulty with the name of his rival: "Colonel Perronet Thompson—I hope I pronounce his name right." This show of imperturbability, this resort to sarcasm instead of anger, would remain Disraeli's standard response to political attacks, no matter how vicious. The eruptive rage of Vivian Grey and Contarini Fleming had been buried deep.

At last, Disraeli's persistence paid off. When the polls closed at the end of July, Disraeli came in second, meaning that he would join Lewis as a Member of Parliament. After five years of effort, he had finally gotten his hands on "the greasy pole." For a man with Disraeli's boundless ambition, however, simply being one of some six hundred and fifty MPs was not enough, and the odds of his making it onto the front bench as a government minister looked very slim. As a Conservative, he belonged to a minority party with little prospect of taking power anytime soon. Worse, Disraeli's reputation—as a dandy, a debtor, an adulterer, an eccentric genius, and a Jew—meant that the Conservative leader, the highly respectable Sir Robert Peel, was hardly likely to promote him over the heads of other, more solid Tory members. Even as he delighted in the pageantry of the opening session, Disraeli must have remembered the prediction he had made in his diary years earlier: "I could rule the House of Commons, although there would be a great prejudice against me at first. It is the most jealous assembly in the world."

Disraeli entered Parliament five years after the passage of the Reform Bill, which supporters and opponents alike believed would transform the House of Commons. In fact, as Disraeli noted in his backward-looking last novel, *Endymion*, "After a short time it was observed that the old material, though at first much less in quantity, had leavened the new mass; that the tone of the former House was imitated and adopted." That tone was still aristocratic, and it suited him perfectly. He never had a high enough opinion of the public to yearn for popular adoration. Unlike Gladstone, whose speeches to huge outdoor crowds became legendary, Disraeli was never at his best on the stump. Instead, like Vivian Grey, he "panted for the Senate"—an exclusive body made up of proud equals, like the patricians of Rome. It was his innate understanding of aristocratic passions—above all, the sense of honor and the longing for distinction—that eventually made Disraeli a master parliamentarian.

The life of an MP at this period in English history was an enviable one. The House of Commons combined the intimacy of a club with the excitement of a theater, and its activities and personalities dominated English life to an extraordinary degree. While the House was in session, from February to August, London society enjoyed its "season." When it broke up, the rich and fashionable dispersed to their country houses for an autumn of hunting and paying visits. Only occasionally was the pattern broken by a special fall session, when there was some pressing business. The sittings of the House began in the late afternoon and often lasted until after midnight, sometimes until four in the morning. Such a schedule increased the sense of drama and urgency during important debates, and Disraeli would often return home at dawn too worked-up to sleep, like an actor after a performance. Indeed, individual speeches could often last longer than a play. A fellow MP congratulated Disraeli after one such speech: "It lasted, they say, three hours, and when it was over I wished it to last three hours more." Outside the House, too, there was an endless appetite for oratory, and detailed reports of parliamentary speeches filled the front pages of newspapers.

Yet a fraternal feeling in the House, a sense that members were all gentlemen together, also allowed for a certain freedom and even levity. In his diary, Lord Stanley frequently remarks on members showing up dead drunk or playing practical jokes on one another. Disraeli himself remembered one moment when the House suddenly turned into the kind of private club where gentlemen told dirty stories. A member

> brought forward once a case of some prisoner, whose wife was not permitted to visit him in prison with free ingress & egress. He said "Things have come to a pretty pass in this country when an Englishman may not have his wife backwards & forwards." The shout of laughter in the House was electrical. Sir Robert Peel, who was naturally a hearty laugher, entirely lost his

habitual self-control, & leant down his head in con-
vulsions.

After a lifetime spent on the margins of English society,
Disraeli reveled in the sense of belonging, at last, to the
elite. He had never considered literary fame an adequate
substitute for parliamentary fame, and he would have sec-
onded the feelings of the anonymous MP quoted by Walter
Bagehot in his classic study *The English Constitution:* " 'I
wrote books,' we have heard of a man saying, 'for twenty
years, and I was nobody; I got into Parliament, and before I
had taken my seat I had become somebody.' " The same
excited pride can be found in Disraeli's letters to Sarah, who
remained his most important confidant. Writing her about
the crowds at the opening session of 1837, when the new
queen met Parliament for the first time, he crowed: "the
moment the magical words 'Member of Parliament' were
uttered all the authorities came to our assistance, all gave
way, and we passed everywhere."

New members usually preferred to be seen and not heard;
but discretion was never Disraeli's way, and he chose the
occasion for his maiden speech with typical rashness. He
rose to speak for the first time in the middle of a debate on
Irish issues, immediately following his archenemy, Daniel
O'Connell. The result could have been foreseen. As soon as
Disraeli got started, a chorus of boos from O'Connell's Irish
supporters drowned him out. He tried several times to go on
with his flowery speech, but each time he was overpowered

by catcalls and the sound of stomping feet. Finally giving up, he made his voice heard over the din with a vow that became famous: "I sit down now, but the time will come when you will hear me."

The fiasco seemed to reprise, in miniature, the whole course of Disraeli's career so far. Once again, his imagination of huge instant success set him up for humiliating failure. But like his earlier setbacks, this one only reinforced Disraeli's iron resolve. He acknowledged to Sarah that "my debut was a *failure*, so far that I could not succeed in gaining an opportunity of saying what I intended; but the failure was not occasioned by my breaking down or any incompetency on my part, but from the physical powers of my adversaries." If he had not managed to finish his speech, at least he got the House's attention, and "next to undoubted success," he assured Sarah, "the best thing is to make a great noise."

During his first year in Parliament, however, Disraeli did not make a great noise. Instead, he restricted himself to low-key, well-thought-out remarks on complex issues like copyright law, gradually earning the respect of the House. He was especially alert to the impression his Jewishness made on his colleagues and was relieved to find it generally passed over in silence. In his very first weeks in Parliament, Disraeli wrote Sarah about a debate "which turned out to be the Jew question by a sidewind." The issue of Jewish emancipation arose during the debate on a bill to allow Quakers to hold local offices without swearing an oath, when one MP tried to have the exemption extended to Jews as well. Disraeli was to be a staunch champion of the Jewish cause, but on this occasion he joined the majority in voting against the proposal, which would have meant using a technicality to avoid dealing openly with the "Jew question." "Nobody looked at me," he told Sarah, "and I was not at all uncomfortable, but voted in the majority with the utmost *sangfroid*." He would not have needed the sangfroid, of course, if he had not been uncomfortable; but appearing comfortable was what mattered most.

Now that he was in Parliament, the only things Disraeli needed to put his disreputable past behind him were money and a good marriage. In 1839, he got them both, in the person of Mary Anne Lewis. Wyndham Lewis, his Maidstone colleague, died in March 1838, and Disraeli quickly made it clear to the widowed Mary Anne that he would be happy to take his place. It would be a beneficial transaction for both of them: Mary Anne could keep her position as an MP's wife, while Disraeli's embarrassed finances made him appreciate her substantial income and her house in London.

Put this way, the courtship sounds a little sordid, and it was certainly no passionate romance, like Disraeli's affair with Henrietta Sykes. But during the year Mary Anne spent in mourning, the ground was laid for an intimate and enduring relationship. When Disraeli first met Mary Anne at a party, years earlier, he had not been impressed, describing her to Sarah as "a flirt and a rattle." But she had since become an important supporter of his career, and what mattered even more to Disraeli, a believer in his genius. That kind of devotion was what he always sought in his relationships with women, perhaps because he was trying to make up for what his mother did not provide. For the same reason, Mary Anne's age—she was forty-five, twelve years older—was not a negative in Disraeli's mind. From Sara Austen to Henrietta, he had always been drawn to older, maternal women. Soon he was writing her, "Tell me that you love your child."

Mary Anne's age may have been a recommendation in another sense, too. She had no children by her first husband, and by now it seemed certain that she would never be a mother. Disraeli could be confident of remaining her only "child," enjoying her undivided attention. This also meant that he would not carry on his family line—a consideration that, to most English gentlemen, trumped all others. Yet Disraeli did not seem to mind that his family name might die out with himself. Late in life, in fact, when he was offered the chance to secure a title for his brother Ralph's son—who was named Coningsby, in honor of Disraeli's novel—he refused several times.

Inevitably, Disraeli's lack of concern with carrying on the family name seems connected to his understanding of himself as the "blank page" between Judaism and Christianity. That image evokes the precariousness of Disraeli's position, unable to come down permanently on either side of a religious and psychological divide. But questions of identity and belonging, which he managed to defer for his own lifetime, would demand an answer if he was going to raise a child. As a father, he would have to decide whether he wanted his children to be Englishmen with Jewish ancestors, or Jews who happened to make England their sphere of action. (The third possibility—that being a Jew and being an Englishman need not conflict—was not imaginable in the England of Disraeli's day; even today, perhaps, such freedom of self-definition is possible only in the United States, not Europe.) Marrying Mary Anne guaranteed that such a difficult decision could be forever postponed—that he would remain a glorious exception, rather than having to formulate a rule.

Whatever tensions about money and motive shadowed their courtship were dispelled in February 1839, when a quarrel prompted Disraeli to write Mary Anne a formidably honest letter. "When I first made my advances to you, I was influenced by no romantic feelings," he admitted. "I was not blind to worldly advantages in such an alliance." But he went on to insist, in an oddly chivalrous turn, that Mary Anne's wealth "proved to be much less than I, or the world, imagined." She had an income from her husband's will, which would cease with her death, but no independent fortune. Disraeli was certain he could do better, if he were simply looking to marry for money: "all that society can offer is at my command." What really drew him to Mary Anne was her ability to be the kind of wife he needed—"one whom I

Benjamin Disraeli

Disraeli at the time of his marriage in 1839:
"My nature demands that my life shall be
perpetual love."

could look upon with pride as the partner of my life, who
could sympathise with all my projects and feelings, console
me in the moments of depression, share my hour of triumph, and work with me for our honor and happiness."

One might be tempted to ask, in the words of Richard III,
"Was ever woman in this humour woo'd?/Was ever woman
in this humour won?" But in fact, Disraeli's letter was per-

fectly designed to banish Mary Anne's doubts, and she wrote back: "For God's sake come to me. . . . I will answer all you wish." In a milieu where marriage was always a financial proposition, he had paid her the compliment of being honest about money. At the same time, he made clear that he wanted their marriage to be an emotional partnership, not just a financial one. "Not all the gold of Ophir should ever lead me to the altar," he concluded. "Far different are the qualities which I require in the sweet participator of my existence. My nature demands that my life shall be perpetual love."

With Mary Anne, who combined experience of the world with a loving, admiring nature, this was exactly the right approach to take. "Every woman in society for years has been taking from Dis," she wrote to a friend. "He appreciates better than any man I know the value of a woman who has something to give in return for being given to. . . . Now I want to give and I know how most exactly." As with his sister, Disraeli offered his fiancée the chance to become a partner in the adventure of his career; it was a way of playing on the passion he understood best, ambition. It seems, too, that there was a genuine sexual attraction between them. On one occasion during their courtship, when Mary Anne was coming to visit him, Disraeli wrote in advance to arrange a clandestine moment: "take care to have your hand *ungloved*, when you arrive, so that you may stand by me, and I may hold and clasp and feel your soft delicious hand."

All these elements combined to make the Disraelis' marriage a famously happy one. "Dizzy married me for my money," Mary Anne was known to say, "but if he had the chance again he would marry me for love." As the conservative "family values" of the Victorian era took hold, Disraeli's reputation as a devoted husband went a long way toward rehabilitating his character. Stories of their mutual devotion circulated. The most famous had to do with an incident when Mary Anne, riding with Disraeli on the way to an important debate in the House, accidentally slammed her fingers in the carriage door. Rather than disturb his concentration, she stifled her cry of pain, and kept smiling until he was out of sight.

Disraeli returned this loyalty in his own way. After decades of marriage, he remained a romantic, chivalrous husband. In 1867, when he and Mary Anne were sick and confined to their separate bedrooms, he wrote her a note: their house "has become a hospital, but a hospital with you is worth a palace with anybody else.—Your own D." He stayed devoted to Mary Anne even as she became something of a ridiculous figure in the eyes of society, continuing to dress and flirt like a girl well into her seventies. Matters weren't helped by what a friend called her "natural speeches," which could have a "startling effect." She surprised Disraeli's friends by admitting that she had never known which came first, the Greeks or the Romans. On another occasion, when someone mentioned a certain lady's pale skin, she replied, "Ah, I wish you could only see my Dizzy in his bath! then you would know what a white skin is." But despite such faux pas, Disraeli remained absolutely devoted to the "sweet participator of his existence." Before she died, in 1872, Mary Anne told a friend that "her life had been a long scene of happiness, owing to his love and kindness."

9

When the next general election was called, in 1841, the Tories' moment finally arrived. A decade in power had left the Whigs fractious and unpopular, and the Conservatives—as they were now coming to be known, under the leadership of Sir Robert Peel—won a large majority in the new Parliament. Disraeli was among them, though he had exchanged his old constituency of Maidstone for a new one, Shrewsbury. As before, he did not relish the actual process of campaigning. In his novel *Coningsby*, he expressed his irritation at the politician's eternal bête noire, the undecided voter: "If you seek their suffrage during the canvass, they reply, that the writ not having come down, the day of election is not yet fixed. If you call again to inform them that the writ has arrived, they rejoin, that after all there may not be a contest. If you call a third time, half dead with fatigue, to give them friendly notice that both you and your rival have pledged yourselves to go to the polls, they twitch their trousers, rub their hands, and with a dull grin observe, 'Well, sir, we shall see.' "

After winning reelection, however, Disraeli faced a more important challenge. He had never wanted to be a mere backbencher; now that his party was in power, he urgently wanted an office. But as details about the composition of Peel's government filtered out, it became clear that Disraeli was not going to be included. He was not too proud to beg, and he wrote to Peel in abject tones: "I have had to struggle against a storm of political hate and malice which few men ever experienced, from the moment . . . I enrolled myself under your banner, and I have only been sustained under these trials by the conviction that the day would come when the foremost man of the country would publicly testify that he had some respect for my ability and my character." Even Mary Anne did her part, reminding Peel (in a letter Disraeli apparently never saw) that her late husband had spent a fortune on the party's behalf.

But it was to no avail. Peel's new government included three future prime ministers, Gladstone among them, but there was no place in it for Disraeli. Despite all he had managed to accomplish, he had not won the trust of the leaders of the Tory Party; he remained a brilliant outsider. Worse, there was no obvious way he could remedy the situation. Peel was a strong prime minister with a large majority, and it seemed likely that he would dominate the party for years, maybe decades to come. All the while, the members of his government would be accumulating influence and experience, so that even after Peel left the scene, his followers would monopolize the Tory leadership. Disraeli's political career, launched with such difficulty, had already reached a dead end.

But Disraeli's early failures taught him to cultivate

patience and ingenuity. Once again, he reacted to disappointment by reaffirming his ambition. If he could not win the distinction he wanted as a politician, he could at least return to his first calling, writing. The trilogy of novels Disraeli produced in the mid-1840s marked an important advance on his early work. He was no longer fantasizing about power, as he had in *Contarini Fleming* and *Alroy;* he was now strategizing for it, deliberately using his writing to advance his own claims to political leadership. Under the cover of fiction, he bitterly criticized Peel, mocked the unimaginative hacks who ran the Tory Party, and knowingly satirized the whole spectacle of English political life. At the same time, he presented a romantic vision of Toryism as it could be, an organic renewal of England's best traditions. In the 1830s, he had employed the freedom of the novelist to re-create Jewish history as he believed it should have been, even if neither the facts nor his readers agreed; in his novels of the 1840s, he was to do the same with English history.

The themes of Disraeli's political novels reflected a shift in his own allegiances. Barred from the Tory leadership, he was eager to define some sort of role for himself in the new Parliament. He found his opportunity in the tiny faction of new MPs who were making a name for themselves under the banner of Young England. John Manners and George Smythe, the group's chief members, had come into Parliament together after years of friendship at Eton and Cambridge. As the sons of noblemen, they had a personal stake in the question that occupied Disraeli from the beginning of his career as a Tory: How could the English aristocracy justify its privileges in a democratic age?

No question was more pressing in the England of the 1840s, where the social costs of urbanization and industrialization were becoming impossible to ignore. The Reform Bill of 1832, which had redressed some of the grievances of the middle class, did nothing for poor farmers and workers, whose living conditions were growing worse and worse. In the late 1830s, the Chartist Movement emerged to demand major constitutional changes that would make Parliament more responsive to the needs of the people. The six points of the People's Charter, from which the movement took its name, included universal male suffrage, equal electoral districts, and payment of MPs. Today, all of these seem like matters of course; but at the time, Chartism looked to the governing class like a threatening omen of mob rule. In 1839, when the Chartists delivered a petition bearing more than a million signatures to Parliament, Whigs and Tories joined in refusing to consider it. Another petition, this one with more than three million names, was rejected in 1842, whereupon strikes broke out around the country. This prompted a government crackdown and the arrest of the main Chartist leaders, breaking the back of the largest democratic movement yet seen in Britain.

At the same time, writers of all ideological stripes were attacking the abuses of Victorian society, creating a new genre of books devoted to "the condition of England." In 1843, the authoritarian conservative Thomas Carlyle published *Past and Present*, a jeremiad against soulless capitalism: "the working body of this rich English Nation has sunk or is fast sinking into a state, to which, all sides of it considered, there was literally never any parallel." He compared Victorian Britain to Midas, who "longed for gold, and insulted the Olympians. He got gold, so that whatsoever he touched became gold,—and he, with his long ears, was little the better for it." Carlyle's critique, though not his conclusions, was echoed by Friedrich Engels, who as a factory manager in Manchester had a front-row seat at the Industrial Revolution. His report, *The Condition of the Working Class in England*, published in 1845, depicted the English proletariat as the "highest and most unconcealed pinnacle of the social misery existing in our day." Only a revolution, he concluded, could bring an end to "the social war, the war of all against all," whose casualties he saw in the teeming London streets.

In these same years, Young England, too, was developing a critique of laissez-faire capitalism, which would find its fullest expression in Disraeli's novels. Their proposed remedy for the condition of England, however, was the opposite of Engels's: instead of advancing to socialism, they hoped to return to feudalism, or at least their own idealized version of it. The virtue of feudalism, in the eyes of Young England, was that it linked privileges with duties. While the capitalist simply exploited the laborer, the nobleman was responsible for the welfare of his dependents. At times, the group's affection for the Middle Ages could seem absurd, as when Smythe suggested reviving the medieval practice of royal "touching" to cure scrofula, the "King's Evil." But the basic political insight of Young England—that triumphant middle-class liberalism could only be defeated by an alliance of the upper and lower classes, in the name of traditional English values—was one that Disraeli took very seriously. Add the fact that Smythe and Manners were born with all the advantages Disraeli lacked, and Young England's appeal for the middle-aged politician became irresistible.

Starting in 1843, Disraeli would use the movement as the inspiration for a series of novels. *Coningsby*, *Sybil*, and *Tancred* each deals with the education of a young, well-meaning nobleman, whose high ideals come into conflict with the cynicism and impotence of English politics. This dynamic allows Disraeli to criticize English society with all the fury of a radical, while still insisting that the ills he diagnoses can only be cured by conservative means. To improve the condition of England would not require dispossessing the rich or enfranchising the poor, as Engels urged and Disraeli's fellow Tories feared. On the contrary, it would mean empowering the rich and teaching the poor to trust their betters. As Egremont, the aristocratic hero of *Sybil*, tells the novel's working-class heroine:

> "The people are not strong; the people never can be strong. Their attempts at self-vindication will end only in their suffering and confusion. . . . The new generation of the aristocracy of England are not tyrants, not oppressors, Sybil, as you persist in believing. Their

intelligence, better than that, their hearts, are open to the responsibility of their position. . . . They are the natural leaders of the people, Sybil; believe me, they are the only ones."

Even at the time, such a message looked too much like wishful thinking to be taken quite seriously. The momentum of the Victorian age was forward toward democracy, not backward toward feudalism, and the comforting dreams of Young England could do nothing to stop it. The movement was, in George Eliot's view, an attempt "to grow fidelity and veneration as we grow turnips, by an artificial system of manure." But if Disraeli's romantic Toryism was poor politics, it was imaginatively alive. In fact, he echoed all the great Victorian writers—Dickens, Carlyle, Arnold, Eliot herself—in his insistence that material progress was doing damage to England's soul. These sages agreed that their materialistic society sorely needed to cultivate the spiritual virtues of compassion, reverence, and imagination. All of them could have endorsed what Disraeli wrote in *Sybil:* "a spirit of rapacious covetousness, desecrating all the humanities of life, has been the besetting sin of England."

But while Disraeli's social criticism is what gives these novels their continuing life, he always stops short of suggesting that actual social conflict is inevitable, and maybe even desirable. His romantic Toryism does not allow him to acknowledge that there may be irreconcilable differences between rich and poor, or that the privileges of the nobleman must be curtailed if the workingman is to be enfranchised. At the same time, his conventional sense of novelistic form compels Disraeli to impose a happy ending on all his characters. The result is that *Coningsby* and *Sybil*, which read for much of their length like protest novels, are forced to end like comedies—that is, with a wedding.

In *Coningsby*, the salvific marriage is between Coningsby, the idealistic grandson of the reactionary Lord Monmouth, and Edith, the daughter of Millbank, an industrial magnate. Their families represent the ingrained class antagonisms of the age—the hidebound aristocracy butting heads with the rising middle class—and neither Monmouth nor Millbank approves of the young people's love. But Coningsby is a member of "The New Generation," as the novel's subtitle proclaims, and he recognizes that the only chance of regenerating England lies in a union of these two powerful classes.

The romance of Coningsby and Edith, then, becomes an allegory of political reconciliation. When Monmouth, irritated by his grandson's political independence, disinherits him, it is Millbank who comes to the rescue, allowing Coningsby to take his own seat in Parliament. An enlightened middle class, Disraeli suggests, will embrace the leadership of the aristocracy, while the aristocracy will use its power for the good of the middle class—as Coningsby does when he rescues Edith's brother from drowning. The novel ends with a series of questions about the young couple's fate, which are also challenges to Disraeli's readers: "Will they maintain in august assemblies and high places the great truths which, in study and in solitude, they have embraced? . . . Will they . . . sensible of the greatness of their position, recognise the greatness of their duties?"

This kind of piety, however, is not the novel's dominant tone; if it were, *Coningsby* would not have remained Disraeli's most popular work. What makes the book so entertaining is, rather, the spirit of Vivian Grey, witty and malicious, turned loose on the shabby spectacle of English politics. In his early novels, Disraeli had not known enough about the practice of politics to write about it convincingly; his ambition was real, but his schemes were fantastic. Now, after years in Parliament, Disraeli knew firsthand how parties worked and how elections were fought. Yet he remained reckless enough, and idealistic enough, to mock the institutions that sheltered him. This mockery finds its focus in Tadpole and Taper, Tory timeservers who wouldn't recognize a great principle if it bit them. "£1,200 per annum, paid quarterly, is their idea of political science and human nature," Disraeli writes. "To receive £1,200 per annum is government; to try to receive £1,200 per annum is opposition; to wish to receive £1,200 per annum is ambition."

Disraeli is daring enough to suggest that the spirit of Tadpolism reaches to the very top of the Tory Party, to his own chief, Peel. He is always willing to interrupt the story in *Coningsby* for a disquisition on the state of party politics, and these have a feline tendency to circle around to the shortcomings of Peel. The prime minister, Disraeli writes, has tried to "construct a party without principles," and the "inevitable consequence has been Political Infidelity." Conservatism is nothing more than a party label, with no principle behind it. "There was indeed a considerable shouting about what they called Conservative principles," Disraeli observes, "but the awkward question naturally arose, What will you conserve? The prerogatives of the Crown, provided they are not exercised; the independence of the House of Lords, provided it is not asserted; the Ecclesiastical estate, provided it is regulated by a commission of laymen. Everything, in short, that is established, as long as it is a phrase and not a fact." Disraeli's whole critique of Peel's Conservatism is summed up in a famous thrust: " 'A sound Conservative government,' said Taper, musingly. 'I understand: Tory men and Whig measures.' "

Peel was beginning to see what kind of an enemy he had made. Disraeli continued the assault in *Sybil*, which appeared the year after *Coningsby*. Now he actually brings "the gentleman in Downing Street" onstage, where he is shown instructing his secretary, Mr. Hoaxem, to make contradictory promises to a group of farmers and a group of manufacturers. "Be 'frank and explicit,' " Peel advises; "that is the right line to take when you wish to conceal your own mind and to confuse the minds of others." Elsewhere in the novel, Disraeli extends his critique of his own party, insisting that Peel's brand of Toryism has nothing in common with the traditional Tory philosophy except the name. "But we forget, Sir Robert Peel is not the leader of the Tory party," he writes. "In a parliamentary sense, that great party has ceased to exist." If Disraeli promises that "Toryism will yet rise from the tomb," he has in mind a very different brand of Toryism, based on the principle "that power has only one duty: to secure the social welfare of the people."

Disraeli's active concern for the working class was one of the most original features of his version of Conservatism, and one of the most influential. It marked him out not just from the bulk of the Tories, who were men of property and rank, but also from the Whigs, whose sympathies lay with middle-class employers, not their hard-pressed employees. In 1839, Disraeli voted, along with most of his colleagues, against receiving the Chartist petition. But he was surprisingly supportive of the Chartist cause, and he was one of just five MPs to vote for leniency for the arrested leaders. "I am not ashamed to say that I sympathise with millions of my fellow-subjects," he declared. His idiosyncratic views, however, were not likely to make him popular with either Radicals or Conservatives. He did not want the workers enfranchised, as the Chartists demanded; but neither did he want their suffering ignored, as most Tories were happy to do. Instead, he called once again for the nobility to take its paternal place as the guardian of the people's interests. "The aristocracy are the natural leaders of the people," he declared on the floor of the House, "for the aristocracy and the labouring population form the nation."

Sybil offers Disraeli's fullest exposition of this idea. Its hero is Charles Egremont, the younger brother of a lord, who like Coningsby starts out in life as a naive idealist. But while Coningsby's education consisted in a pleasant romance with the daughter of a rich manufacturer, Egremont's is far more difficult and takes him to much darker corners of English society. For Egremont falls in love with Sybil Gerard, the daughter of a Chartist leader, who spends her days visiting the hovels of the poor. Assuming an incognito to win the trust of Sybil and her father, Walter, Egremont is exposed to the horrifying depths of poverty that the Industrial Revolution brought to England. He discovers that "infanticide is practised as extensively and as legally in England as it is on the banks of the Ganges," that in an average industrial town "there are many . . . who are ignorant of their very names; very few who can spell them."

Disraeli took his statistics and examples from government reports, and he insisted that he had not exaggerated the plight of the poor. On the contrary, he "found the absolute necessity of suppressing much that is genuine. For so little do we know of the state of our own country, that the air of improbability which the whole truth would inevitably throw over these pages, might deter some from their perusal." Even more than the suffering of the poor, what *Sybil* brings home to the reader is the impassable gulf dividing the haves and the have-nots in Victorian England. They are, according to the novel's subtitle, "two nations" living side by side in mutual ignorance. In the novel's most famous passage, this truth is revealed to Egremont by a Chartist agitator:

"Well, society may be in its infancy," said Egremont, slightly smiling; "but, say what you like, our Queen reigns over the greatest nation that ever existed."

"Which nation?" asked the younger stranger, "for she reigns over two."

The stranger paused; Egremont was silent, but looked inquiringly.

"Yes," resumed the younger stranger after a moment's interval. "Two nations; between whom there is no intercourse and no sympathy; who are as ignorant of each other's habits, thoughts, and feelings, as if they were dwellers in different zones, or inhabitants of different planets; who are formed by a different breeding, are fed by a different food, are ordered by different manners, and are not governed by the same laws."

"You speak of—" said Egremont, hesitatingly.

"The Rich and the Poor."

After *Sybil*, "the two nations" became a popular shorthand for the problem facing Britain. It was a deeply Disraelian way of framing the social question, drawing on the powerful charge that the word "nation" always held for him. For Engels, the bourgeoisie and the proletariat were enemies by definition; the class struggle was a zero-sum game and could only be resolved by the victory of one side. For Disraeli, Victorian Britain was rather a nation split in two, whose only possible salvation lay in reconciliation. What most shocks him, in *Sybil*, is not the exploitation of one class by another, but the alienation of the poor from the English privileges and traditions that are rightfully theirs.

These are, significantly, not just economic privileges but also cultural and religious ones. In one memorable scene, an ignorant but well-meaning girl declares that she believes "in our Lord and Saviour Pontius Pilate, who was crucified to save our sins; and in Moses, Goliath, and the rest of the Apostles"—a parody of the Creed designed to shock the conscience of a nation that took its Christian identity very seriously. The irony is that this vision of England as it should be—united in its interests, traditions, and beliefs— came from a writer who could never be fully accepted by such an England, and indeed never was. In fiction as in politics, Disraeli felt the power of nationhood all the more acutely because he did not really belong to the nation he lived in—and the nation he might have belonged to, the Jewish nation he imagined in *Alroy* and *Tancred*, did not exist.

If Disraeli presents the problem of "the two nations" in stark terms, however, he once again shies away from a realistic analysis of how it might be solved. The novel culminates in a mob uprising, in which Egremont's reactionary brother is killed along with Sybil's father. But this nightmarish scene immediately gives way to another of Disraeli's happy endings. Not only does Egremont inherit his brother's title but Sybil, it turns out, is the heiress to a long-lost estate. After all Disraeli has shown the reader of the suffering of the poor and the callousness of the rich, this denouement feels not just artificial but offensive. The marriage of Sybil and Egremont is meant to symbolize the reconciliation of the nobility and the working class; but Disraeli, by surreptitiously promoting Sybil to the nobility, essentially papers over the class conflict he has spent the whole novel dramatizing.

This is just the kind of wishful thinking that led George Eliot to dismiss Young England as "aristocratic dilettantism." Engels, naturally, was still harsher about "the philanthropic Tories, who have recently constituted themselves 'Young England.' " Mentioning Disraeli and others by name, he sneered, "the hope of 'Young England' is a restoration of the old 'merry England.' . . . The object is of course unattainable and ridiculous, a satire upon all historic development." At most, he was willing to give the group credit for recognizing "the vileness of our present condition."

But Engels was already committed to the violent overthrow of English society. Disraeli, who had spent his whole life trying to make a place for himself in that society, was not so eager to write it off. In an influential essay on the conservative thought of Samuel Taylor Coleridge, the liberal philosopher John Stuart Mill wrote that the only way the Tories could defend England's institutions was to rethink them from the ground up: "What it is that we have a right to expect from things established—which they are bound to do for us, as the justification of their being established; so that they may be recalled to it and compelled to do it, or the impossibility of their any longer doing it may be conclusively manifested." That is exactly the task Disraeli took up in *Coningsby* and *Sybil*, although his answers did not succeed in winning over the liberal intelligentsia. In 1847, the leading Whig journal, the *Edinburgh Review*, dismissed his political novels in a long, withering review, arguing that Disraeli was opposed to "the progress of civilization, the development of human intelligence"—in short, everything for which humanity had "been yearning, and fighting, and praying for the last three centuries." The critics were right that the nineteenth century could never go back to the kind of benevolent feudalism that existed, perhaps, nowhere but in the imagination of Young England. But in his fiction, Disraeli at least managed to put on record his dream of what England should be.

10

Comparing Disraeli's political novels of the 1840s to his autobiographical novels of the 1830s, it is immediately obvious that there has been a change in focus. Contarini Fleming and Vivian Grey were the author's fantasy selves, and writing about them was essentially a way to gratify in imagination the ambition that remained stifled in real life. Coningsby and Egremont, however, are clearly not based on Disraeli himself: they are too naive, and too uncomplicatedly English, to be versions of their creator. Their originals, rather, were the young men of Young England—earnest, slightly ridiculous figures like Smythe and Manners, whom Disraeli liked but did not want to emulate. Where, then, does Disraeli himself figure in his political novels? The question might be phrased another way: What place is there for a brilliant, ambitious Jew in the England of Disraeli's imagination, led as it is by stalwart English lords?

The answer is that Disraeli did write himself into these novels, but not in the role of the hero. Instead, he created the most influential and provocative of his fictional avatars: Sidonia, the international Jewish mastermind. Sidonia plays a minor role in *Sybil* and *Tancred*, a major one in *Coningsby*, but in all three novels he is crucial to Disraeli's design. For it is

Sidonia who allowed Disraeli to imagine a place for himself in the councils of power, at a moment in his career when parliamentary success seemed further off than ever. At the same time, Sidonia is the mouthpiece through which he asserts his continuing belief in the dignity of the Jewish people. Disraeli had long since abandoned the dream of being Alroy, a Jewish national leader; but in Sidonia, he clung to the hope that Jewishness could bring another kind of power and pride.

The key to Sidonia's power, however, is that it is always exerted behind the scenes. Disraeli emphasizes this point from the character's first appearance, at an inn where he and Coningsby have taken refuge from a rainstorm. Sidonia makes a powerful impression on the young Englishman, thanks to his foreign and intellectual appearance: he is "pale, with an impressive brow, and dark eyes of great intelligence." It is point for point the way strangers always described Disraeli himself—remember a witness's description of him in 1835, "lividly pale, and from beneath two finely-arched eyebrows blazed out a pair of intensely black eyes." Sidonia's demeanor, too, is the one Disraeli was at pains to cultivate: "If his address had any fault in it, it was rather a deficiency of earnestness. A slight spirit of mockery played over his speech even when you deemed him most serious."

Where Vivian and Contarini were passionately earnest, Sidonia remains ironically detached. And the reason for his detachment, it soon appears, is that he is condemned to remain outside the sphere of political life. He enchants Coningsby with a long disquisition on the power of individual will, reeling off a catalogue of heroes who made their mark when no older than Coningsby himself. "Do not suppose," he says, "that I hold that youth is genius; all that I say is, that genius, when young, is divine." He strongly intimates that a genius is what the present age needs: "From the throne to the hovel all call for a guide." Naturally, Coningsby wonders why Sidonia—who, "without the slightest air of pretension or parade . . . seemed to know everybody as well as everything"—does not aspire to be the age's guide himself. The answer becomes clear in a chapter-ending flourish:

> "Your mind at least is nurtured with great thoughts," said Coningsby; "your actions should be heroic."
>
> "Action is not for me," said the stranger; "I am of that faith that the Apostles professed before they followed their master."
>
> He vaulted into his saddle, "the Daughter of the Star" bounded away as if she scented the air of the Desert from which she and her rider had alike sprung, and Coningsby remained in profound meditation.

There is something very Hollywood about the scene—you can practically hear the soundtrack as Sidonia, the man of mystery, gallops into the night. But the purpose of the exchange is serious enough. Because he is a Jew, Disraeli implies, Sidonia can never engage in a life of heroic action. Most obviously, he cannot run for Parliament, since Jews were still unable to take the required oath. But there is more to Sidonia's fate than a mere legal restriction. Later in the novel, when Disraeli gives us his history, we learn that his learning and wealth have left him utterly jaded: "Sidonia nevertheless looked upon life with a glance rather of curiosity than content. His religion walled him out from the pursuits of a citizen; his riches deprived him of the stimulating anxieties of a man." He is less than a man in a more intimate sense, too: "He might have discovered that perpetual spring of happiness in the sensibility of the heart. But this was a sealed fountain to Sidonia. In his organization there was a peculiarity, perhaps a great deficiency. He was a man without affections."

In short, Sidonia—who knows everything and enjoys nothing, who seems to have lived longer than his years, who cannot feel human love—is the Wandering Jew. Disraeli has modeled his Jewish hero on this medieval anti-Semitic archetype, the Jew who laughed at Christ on Calvary and was punished with eternal exile. Deliberately, even if not consciously, Disraeli concentrates in Sidonia all the Christian world's suspicions and fears about Jewish uncanniness.

Yet he does this in a defiant spirit; for Sidonia, despite his limitations, is meant to be a figure of great power and glamour. The other archetype that goes into his creation is a modern one—the international Jew, who is nowhere in office but controls every government from behind the scenes. In particular, Sidonia sounds like a Rothschild, or what the public believed the Rothschilds to be. "Europe did require money, and Sidonia was ready to lend it to Europe," Disraeli writes. "France wanted some; Austria more; Prussia a little; Russia a few millions. Sidonia could furnish them all. . . . He was lord and master of the money-market of the world, and of course virtually lord and master of everything else."

By the time he wrote *Coningsby*, Disraeli was acquainted with the actual Rothschilds. As he became one of the most famous Jews in England, he inevitably entered their stratospheric social orbit. In time, his friendship with Baron Lionel de Rothschild, the head of the family's English branch, would become significant to Disraeli both personally and politically. When Hannah Rothschild, Lionel's niece and the richest heiress in England, married Lord Rosebery, a future prime minister, in 1878, it was Disraeli who gave the bride away. More consequentially, Disraeli relied on the family's business contacts for news about Continental politics, often irritating his colleagues by implying that the Rothschilds had better information than Britain's ambassadors. When he was prime minister, his ability to secure a huge loan from the Rothschilds enabled him to pull off one of his greatest coups, the purchase of a share in the Suez Canal Company for the British government.

In the mid-1840s, this intimacy was still in the future. But Disraeli already knew the Rothschilds well enough and knew enough about them, to realize that Lionel was not in the least like Sidonia. Far from working British statesmen like marionettes from behind the scenes, Lionel was head of the campaign to allow Jews to sit in Parliament—a modest goal that, despite the alleged power of the Rothschilds, took decades to achieve. The Rothschild family was, of course, extremely rich, and their bank's central role in international finance gave them great influence. But what they used that influence to achieve was not secret power, but civic equality and social respectability. A seat in Parliament, a stable of racehorses, a fine estate, titled husbands for their daughters—these were the goals of the actual Rothschilds.

If Sidonia wanted much more, that is because he expresses, in a new form, Disraeli's old longing for power. Disraeli gives Sidonia the same genealogy he invented for himself: he is descended from the Jews of Spain, that noble race which allegedly included "two-thirds of the Arragonese nobility." After the Inquisition, when Disraeli's putative ancestors left Spain, Sidonia's remained and became *conversos.* But for three centuries they kept their Judaism alive in secret, and when they left Spain at last, during the Napoleonic Wars, they immediately professed it. This part of the Sidonia legend comes dangerously close to Disraeli's own life: if the Sidonias could pretend to be Christians for three hundred years, the reader might well ask, couldn't Disraeli maintain the same charade for thirty? It is as though Disraeli were teasingly retracting his own conversion, daring his readers to believe that a Jew could ever stop being a Jew.

In fact, Sidonia explains, such a conversion is literally impossible, since Jewishness is not a matter of religion, but of race. "To the unpolluted current of their Caucasian structure, and to the segregating genius of their great Lawgiver," Disraeli writes, "Sidonia ascribed the fact that they had not been long ago absorbed among those mixed races who presume to persecute them, but who periodically wear away and disappear, while their victims still flourish in all the primeval vigour of the pure Asian breed." Racial purity is the key to Jewish survival, and also to Jewish power. Indeed, because the Jews are a pure race and the Anglo-Saxons are not, a Jew like Sidonia has a far nobler lineage than any English aristocrat. "A few centuries back," Sidonia jeers, Englishmen "were tattooed savages." This doctrine allows Disraeli to mock the English peerage with undisguised glee: "An unmixed race of a first-rate organization are the aristocracy of nature. Such excellence is a positive fact; not an imagination, a ceremony, coined by poets, blazoned by cozening heralds, but perceptible in its physical advantages, and in the vigour of its unsullied idiosyncrasy."

Lines like these make it clear why Disraeli found it so imaginatively rewarding to create an alter ego such as Sidonia. It was, at bottom, an act of revenge, the retort of his wounded amour propre upon the society that snubbed and thwarted him. From his earliest years, Disraeli showed in his novels, his pride gave him no rest. He yearned to demonstrate his superiority, first over his schoolmates, then over his countrymen; he was conscious of great gifts and "panted" for the chance to display them. Yet all his life, as he told Peel, he had struggled against "a storm of political hate and malice." And while Disraeli's Jewishness was not the only cause of that hatred, it was almost always an element in it. From the boys who yelled "no stranger" at Vivian Grey, to the *Punch* jokers who gave Disraeli the accent of an East End ragman, and down to the end of his life, his Jewishness was thrown in his face as an insult. He took care that these taunts should not be seen to upset him, cultivating an air of superiority that in turn became its own kind of provocation.

But on the page, in creating Sidonia, Disraeli could let himself go. Here was a Jew who was better-born than the Tory gentlemen and richer than the Whig magnates; who didn't need to struggle for power in Parliament, because he wielded power greater than any Parliament. Above all, Sidonia was a Jew who could never be insulted. "Sidonia, indeed, was exactly the character who would be welcomed in our circles," Disraeli writes. "His immense wealth, his unrivalled social knowledge, his clear, vigorous intellect, the severe simplicity of his manners, frank, but neither claiming nor brooking familiarity, and his devotion to field-sports . . . were all circumstances and qualities which the English appreciate and admire; and it may be fairly said of Sidonia that few men were more popular, and none less understood."

It is only by seeing Sidonia in this light, as Disraeli's compensatory fantasy, that we can understand the appeal of such a character to his imagination. For by now, after a century and a half of Jewish history that Disraeli could never have foreseen, Sidonia looks like nothing so much as an anti-Semitic hate figure. It is amazing, in fact, how Disraeli manages to combine in this one character every malicious slander and paranoid fear that the anti-Semitic imagination can breed. Sidonia, as we have seen, is the international banker who is "lord and master" of the world. But he is also the spider in the web of revolutionary conspiracy: "There was not an adventurer in Europe with whom he was not familiar. No minister of state had such communication with secret agents and political spies as Sidonia. He held relations with all the clever outcasts of the world." He is sexually unwholesome: "Something of the old Oriental vein influenced him in his carriage toward women. He was oftener behind the scenes of the Opera House than in his box; he delighted, too, in the society of *hetairai*"—that is, courtesans. He reveals that Jews are responsible for every movement of history: "You never observe a great intellectual movement in Europe in which the Jews do not greatly participate. The first Jesuits were Jews; that mysterious Russian diplomacy which so alarms Western Europe is organised and principally carried on by Jews; that mighty revolution which is at this moment preparing in Germany . . . is entirely developing under the auspices of Jews." He even gives Coningsby a list of famous men who are secretly Jews, including Napoléon's Marshals Soult and Masséna ("his real name was Manasseh").

With a few slight changes, you could easily turn the Sidonia scenes in *Coningsby* and *Tancred* into an anti-Semitic tract to rival *The Protocols of the Elders of Zion*. And, as a matter of fact, the most vicious anti-Semites of the late nineteenth century all reprised Disraeli's ideas, sometimes giving him explicit credit. Karl Eugen Duehring, one of the major "theorists" of anti-Semitism, was happy to agree with Sidonia's racial doctrines: "the Jews are to be defined solely on the basis of race, and not on the basis of religion." Wilhelm Marr, who coined the word "anti-Semitism," accepted Disraeli's suggestion that Jews ran the world from behind the scenes, and named him as the prime example: "the Semite Disraeli . . . holds in his vest-pocket the key to war and peace in the Orient."

The infamous anti-Semitic work by Houston Stewart Chamberlain, *The Foundations of the Nineteenth Century*—which held a privileged place in the Nazi canon—is premised on Sidonia's belief that racial "excellence is a positive fact." In *Tancred*, Sidonia asks, "What is individual character but the personification of race, its perfection and choice exemplar?" Chamberlain agrees wholeheartedly: "Nothing is so convincing as the consciousness of the possession of race," he writes. "The man who belongs to a distinct, pure race, never loses the sense of it." Quite sincerely, this leading Jew-hater gives credit to Disraeli for revealing the truth about Jews: "In days when so much nonsense is talked concerning this question, let Disraeli teach us that the whole significance of Judaism lies in its purity of race, that this alone gives it power and duration." And there is a footnote: "See the novels *Tancred* and *Coningsby*. In the latter Sidonia says: 'Race is everything; there is no other truth. And every race must fall which carelessly suffers its blood to become mixed.' "

Could Disraeli have foreseen the use that the enemies of

the Jews would make of his words? By the end of his life, the possibility began to dawn on him: in his novel *Lothair*, published in 1870, he would uneasily portray a votary of the new racial anti-Semitism. But in the 1840s, the prospect was too remote for Disraeli to consider. The pseudoscience of race, which Sidonia invokes so fluently, was just becoming popular—Arthur de Gobineau's influential *Essay on the Inequality of the Human Races* would be published in the early 1850s—and it appealed to Disraeli for obvious reasons. As a convert to Christianity, the idea of race gave him the vocabulary he needed to assert that he was still a Jew. It also allowed him to turn the English obsession with pedigree to his own advantage. Instead of belonging to a low caste, he could insist, he was the descendant of a pure and ancient bloodline. This made sense in an English context where anti-Semitism was based primarily on contempt—the kind of contempt George Eliot complained about in a letter to Harriet Beecher Stowe: "Not only towards the Jews, but towards all oriental peoples with whom we English come in contact, a spirit of arrogance and contemptuous dictatorialness is observable which has become a national disgrace to us."

By the end of Disraeli's life, however, anti-Semitism had mutated into something much more virulent, based no longer on contempt but on fear and hatred. The myth of Jewish superiority, which Disraeli had advanced to counter the fact of social inferiority, now interacted with the paranoid suspicions of anti-Semites to disastrous effect. Indeed, of all the strokes of good luck that made Disraeli's career possible, one of the most conspicuous was the fact that he died in 1881—just one year before the promulgation of the oppressive May Laws in Russia led to a surge of Jewish emigration, bringing the Jewish question to the forefront of politics and fueling anti-Semitic movements across Europe. If Disraeli had been born half a generation later, he might have found himself prime minister of England while the Dreyfus Affair convulsed France, or negotiating war and peace with Russia as the tsar's state-sponsored pogroms terrorized the Pale of Settlement. In such circumstances, the competing demands of Disraeli's Jewish and English loyalties, which he managed to finesse for most of his career, might have become intolerable, both electorally and psychologically.

It is true that, even as anti-Semitism flourished in Germany and France, it would never achieve much currency in Disraeli's homeland. Yet even in England, the situation of the Jews became much more difficult after 1881, as refugees from Poland began to transform the demographic profile of English Jewry. In the year of Disraeli's death, the Jewish population of Britain was approximately sixty-five thousand; thirty years later it had tripled, and the East End of London had taken on the appearance of a Jewish slum. Occasional anti-Jewish riots, and a growing movement to restrict Jewish immigration, led to a new feeling of insecurity among British Jews. In 1899, the rabbi of London's Great Synagogue warned his congregants that the Dreyfus Affair was the "handwriting on the wall" for Jews, a sign that they needed "to be more cautious and circumspect than ever before." It was fortunate for the creator of Sidonia that he was no longer alive to hear that warning.

The Jews, Disraeli argues in Sidonia's voice, are superior to every other people in intellect, wealth, power, and blood. But there is one more advantage for Sidonia to insist on, and in Disraeli's political vision, it is the most important. For the Jews are also the exclusive bearers of divine revelation, not just in the biblical past, but in the nineteenth century as well. In *Coningsby* and *Sybil*, Disraeli had written that English society could only be saved by a spiritual regeneration. Now, in *Tancred*, he goes on to argue that regeneration can only come from what his father called "the genius of Judaism." It is Disraeli's most daring attempt to bridge the gulf between England, the Israel of his imagination, and Israel, which he presents as England's spiritual and moral tutor. In Disraeli's poetic vision, however, the genius of Judaism has little to do with the religion actually practiced by Jews. It is, rather, a mystical spirit that dwells in the Near East, and which inspired all three of the great monotheistic religions. Only by making contact with that spirit—which Disraeli names, in another famous phrase, "the great Asian mystery"—can England renew its own greatness.

In *Tancred*, which he began to write immediately after finishing *Sybil* in 1845, Disraeli's hero is once again an idealistic young nobleman just entering public life. Tancred is the only son of the Duke and Duchess of Bellamont, and as the novel opens his family is preparing to celebrate his twenty-first birthday with a grand party. But where Coningsby was drawn to politics and Egremont to social reform, Tancred is interested mainly in religion. And the religious institutions of Victorian England, he finds to his despair, can offer neither guidance nor inspiration. When his conventional parents, unable to fathom his spiritual urgency, send Tancred to a bishop for advice, the result is a dialogue of the deaf:

> "There is a great spirit rising in the Church," observed the bishop, with thoughtful solemnity; "a great and excellent spirit. The Church of 1845 is not the Church of 1745. We must remember that; we know not what may happen. We shall soon see a bishop at Manchester."
>
> "But I want to see an angel at Manchester."
>
> "An angel!"
>
> "Why not? Why should there not be heavenly messengers, when heavenly messages are most wanted?"

What Tancred really wants is to become a Kierkegaardian knight of faith. He is not content to be a Christian in name only but must experience the divine directly. His mission is already implicit in his name: the original Tancred was one of the leaders of the First Crusade, and his namesake believes that he, too, must see the Holy Land if his questions are to be answered. He cannot believe "that Palestine is like Normandy or Yorkshire, or even Attica or Rome." He tells his baffled parents that he will make a pilgrimage to the Holy Sepulchre: "It is time to restore and renovate our communications with the Most High. I, too, would kneel at that tomb; I, too, surrounded by the holy hills and sacred groves of Jerusalem, would relieve my spirit from the bale that bows it down; would lift up my voice to heaven, and ask, 'What is duty, and what is faith? What ought I to do, and what ought I to believe?' "

The idea that the land of Israel is charged with a mystical power was familiar, as we have seen, from a strand of Christian thought that stretched back to the Puritans. But the notion that a believer must actually go to Jerusalem in order to make contact with God is very far from the doctrines of Christianity, or of Judaism, for that matter. It makes sense only as another expression of Disraeli's Jewish chauvinism, which in *Tancred* becomes a broader spiritual principle. Contrary to the basic premise of monotheism, Disraeli suggests that God speaks only to Semitic peoples and only in the Middle East. Judaism, Christianity, and Islam are Semitic family possessions, shared only grudgingly with the less gifted peoples of the world. The shared origin of the three faiths is far more important than their religious, cultural, and historical differences. All of them participate in "the great Asian mystery," all were inspired by what Disraeli calls "the Angel of Arabia." "Christianity," he writes, "is Judaism for the multitude," and "the Arabs are only Jews upon horseback." (One side benefit of this principle is that Disraeli can identify the

Jews, whom the English despise, with the Arabs, whom the English respect.)

To drive the point home, Disraeli brings back Sidonia, who educates Tancred as he did Coningsby. "I believe that God spoke to Moses on Mount Horeb, and you believe that he was crucified, in the person of Jesus, on Mount Calvary," he explains. "Both were, at least carnally, children of Israel: they spoke Hebrew to the Hebrews. The prophets were only Hebrews; the apostles were only Hebrews. The churches of Asia, which have vanished, were founded by a native Hebrew; and the church of Rome . . . was also founded by a Hebrew." It is Sidonia's old habit of insisting that everyone famous is a Jew, now transposed to the sacred realm: before it was Marshal Soult, now it is Saint Paul. The key to this rhetorical tactic lies in Sidonia's formula, "only Hebrews." To the Christian, of course, what matters about the apostles is not that they were Hebrews, but that they were Christians. To Disraeli, on the other hand, Jewishness or "Semitism" is necessarily prior to any intellectual commitment or spiritual belief. As Sidonia insists, "All is race; there is no other truth."

Armed with this advice, and with a letter of credit from Sidonia, Tancred makes his way to Palestine. Once he arrives, however, the novel takes a strange turn. The young English pilgrim seems to forget that his purpose was to receive sacred guidance for the regeneration of England. Instead, he wanders into a reprise of *Alroy*, a Disraelian fantasy of proto-Zionist power politics. The center of the action shifts from Tancred to Fakredeen, a poor Lebanese prince who is scheming to regain control of his family's lands. In order to buy the weapons he needs, Fakredeen arranges to have the Englishman kidnapped, expecting that his family will pay a large ransom. But he soon falls under the spell of Tancred's grand scheme for the conquest of the whole Middle East. "A man might climb Mount Carmel," Tancred muses, "and utter three words which would bring the Arabs again to Granada, and perhaps further." He is like Lawrence of Arabia, come seventy years too early.

Tancred's sense of mission is confirmed when he visits Mount Sinai and prays to the "Lord God of Israel, Creator of the Universe, ineffable Jehovah!" He is vouchsafed a vision of the Angel of Arabia, who commands him to unite Asia and Europe in a new theocratic order: "The equality of man," the angel proclaims, "can only be accomplished by the sovereignty of God." It is only now that the true meaning of the novel's subtitle, *The New Crusade*, becomes clear. Disraeli does not mean that Tancred should lead a crusade to conquer Palestine for Europe. On the contrary, he believes that the Semitic race, with its genius for religion, must reconquer the decadent, materialistic West. In *The Genius of Judaism*, Isaac D'Israeli had praised the theocratic equality of the biblical commonwealth; now his son dreams of bringing all Europe under that ancient order.

Considered as a political program, theocracy was still more of a nonstarter than the neofeudalism of Young England. In *Coningsby* and *Sybil*, Disraeli suggested turning back the clock of history by three hundred years; in *Tancred*, it is more like three thousand. As a result, the novel can be read as a parody, possibly even a deliberate one, of the romantic Toryism Disraeli spent his career elaborating. The sheer unreality of Tancred's political vision becomes a sign of the futility of reaction in an age of progress. Even Disraeli couldn't come up with a convincing end to his hero's story: the novel breaks off just after Tancred has won his first battle, with the arrival of his parents in Jerusalem.

But *Tancred*, like all Disraeli's best novels, also gave him the chance to dramatize aspects of his own personality and to reckon with the conflicting pressures of his ambition. For if Disraeli sees part of himself in Tancred—the idealistic conservative, seeking to make contact with the living fountain of tradition—he projects a different side in Fakredeen, the utterly unscrupulous politician. Fakredeen, who will do anything to achieve power, is like a more successful and ruthless Vivian Grey:

> He became habituated to the idea that everything could be achieved by dexterity, and that there was no test of conduct except success. To dissemble and to simulate; to conduct confidential negotiations with contending powers and parties at the same time; to be ready to adopt any opinion and to possess none; to fall into the public humour of the moment, and to evade the impending catastrophe; to look upon every man as a tool, and never do anything which had not a definite

though circuitous purpose; these were his political accomplishments; and, while he recognised them as the best means of success, he found in their exercise excitement and delight.

None of Disraeli's enemies could have drawn a more vicious caricature. He even allows Fakredeen to declare, "I am of that religion which gives me a sceptre"—a dangerous line from the pen of a Jewish convert to Christianity. Creating such a character must have gratified Disraeli's native impudence, giving him the chance to parade all his unearnest, un-Victorian qualities before the reader. No wonder *Tancred* baffled the great Victorian critic Leslie Stephen, who regarded it as a "strange phantasmagoria," and was especially dismayed by the way Disraeli seemed "to pray with the mystic and sneer with the politician" at the same time.

But Fakredeen also seems like a kind of self-interrogation, as though Disraeli were asking himself how much truth lay behind his enemies' charges of hypocrisy and opportunism. Finally, Disraeli seems to conclude that Fakredeen's brand of intrigue, though it appeals to one part of his nature, is unbecoming in a truly great statesman. "I do not believe that anything great is ever effected by management," Tancred lectures Fakredeen. "All this intrigue, in which you seem such an adept, might be of some service in a court or in an exclusive senate; but to free a nation you require something more vigorous and more simple."

For all its outrageous theorizing about Judaism, *Tancred* also includes some of Disraeli's most touching and sincere writing about Jews. Just as he had once written *Alroy* to explore his "ideal ambition" of becoming a Jewish national leader, now he uses *Tancred* to imagine the possibility of a Jewish society in Palestine. At times, the novel reads like a Zionist idyll, picturing a world where Jews are not a minority but the majority. There are more Jewish characters in *Tancred* than in any of Disraeli's other books—Jewish merchants and Jewish bandits and Jewish debutantes. Above all there is Eva, the beautiful Jewish woman known as "the Rose of Sharon." As Tancred falls in love with Eva, she raises his consciousness about the injuries Christians do to Jewish dignity:

> "My grandfather is a Bedouin sheikh, chief of one of the most powerful tribes of the desert. My mother was his daughter. He is a Jew; his whole tribe are Jews; they read and obey the five books, live in tents, have thousands of camels, ride horses of the Nedjed breed, and care for nothing except Jehovah, Moses, and their mares. Were they at Jerusalem at the crucifixion, and does the shout of the rabble touch them? Yet my mother marries a Hebrew of the cities, and a man, too, fit to sit on the throne of King Solomon; and a little Christian Yahoor with a round hat, who sells figs at Smyrna, will cross the street if he see her, lest he should be contaminated by the blood of one who cruci-

fied his Saviour; his Saviour being, by his own statement, one of the princes of our royal house. No; I will
never become a Christian, if I am to eat such sand!"

There is a world of difference between this simple pride,
the birthright of a Jew of Palestine, and the shadowy manip-
ulations of Sidonia, the Jew of the Diaspora. It is obvious
that Disraeli's imagination still reveled in the idea of
belonging to a Jewish society, long after he had devoted all of
his energies to succeeding on his own in English society. It is
no coincidence that *Tancred* is also the only novel of Disraeli's in which he describes a Jewish custom in a way that
reflects his own personal experience. Some childhood
memory of celebrating Succoth, probably at a relative's
house in London, must lie behind this passage, which reveals
a side of Disraeli's Jewish feelings that he never exposed
again:

Conceive a being born and bred in the Judenstrasse of
Hamburg or Frankfort, or rather in the purlieus of our
Houndsditch or Minories, born to hereditary insult,
without any education, apparently without a circumstance that can develop the slightest taste, or cherish
the least sentiment for the beautiful, living amid fogs
and filth, never treated with kindness, seldom with justice, occupied with the meanest, if not the vilest, toil,
bargaining for frippery, speculating in usury, existing
forever under the concurrent influence of degrading
causes which would have worn out, long ago, any race

that was not of the unmixed blood of Caucasus, and did not adhere to the laws of Moses; conceive such a being, an object to you of prejudice, dislike, disgust, perhaps hatred. The season arrives, and the mind and heart of that being are filled with images and passions that have been ranked in all ages among the most beautiful and the most genial of human experience. . . . The harvest of the grape in the native regions of the Vine.

He rises early in the morning, goes early to some Whitechapel market, purchases some willow boughs for which he has previously given a commission, and which are brought, probably, from one of the neighbouring rivers of Essex, hastens home, cleans out the yard of his miserable tenement, builds his bower, decks it, even profusely, with the finest flowers and fruits that he can procure, the myrtle and the citron never forgotten, and hangs its roof with variegated lamps. After the service of his synagogue, he sups late with his wife and his children in the open air, as if he were in the pleasant villages of Galilee, beneath its sweet and starry sky.

Perhaps, as he is giving the Keedush, the Hebrew blessing to the Hebrew meal, breaking and distributing the bread, and sanctifying, with a preliminary prayer, the goblet of wine he holds, the very ceremony which the Divine Prince of Israel, nearly two thousand years ago, adopted at the most memorable of all repasts. . . . A party of Anglo-Saxons, very respectable men, ten-pounders, a little elevated it may be, though certainly not in honour of the vintage, pass the house, and words like these are heard:

"I say, Buggins, what's that row?"

"Oh! it's those cursed Jews. We've a lot of 'em here. It is one of their horrible feasts. The Lord Mayor ought to interfere. However, things are not as bad as they used to be; they used always to crucify little boys at these hullabaloos, but now they only eat sausages made of stinking pork."

"To be sure," replies his companion, "we all make progress."

Disraeli's obnoxious theories about "unmixed blood" are here, and so is his Deronda-like recoil from poor Jews who live "amid fogs and filth." But we can also see, in this description, the dignity of actual Jewish life in England, and Disraeli's powerful need to defend the Jews against Christian contempt. Not that he succeeded in changing many English minds: *Punch*, reviewing *Tancred* in an article headlined "The Jewish Champion," simply reiterated the arrogant stupidity of Buggins. "After reading [Disraeli's] last work of *Tancred*," the magazine jeered, "we took quite a fresh view of all the itinerant sons of Israel whom we met in the streets of the Great Metropolis. 'Look at the old clothes man,' said we to ourselves, 'who would think that the unmixed blood of the Caucasus runs through the veins of that individual who has just offered us nine pence for our hat?' " But if Disraeli could not singlehandedly change the way England thought about Jews, at least he could satisfy his own pride, by contrasting noble Jewish traditions with Anglo-Saxon vulgarity. If Disraeli had placed more trust in the realistic description of Jewish life, instead of elaborating a fantasy of Jewish power, he might have left a greater legacy.

11

When Disraeli began writing *Coningsby* in 1843, he was a Tory dissident and permanent backbencher. By the time *Tancred* was published, in 1847, he was one of the leaders of the Tory Party. He owed this unlikely promotion to a political earthquake triggered by the most divisive issue in British politics, the Corn Laws. The same assertive middle class that had forced Parliament to pass the Reform Bill was now demanding the repeal of these protectionist measures, which blocked imports of grain when the price fell below a certain level. To the members of the Anti–Corn Law League, a nationwide pressure group founded in 1839, the law was straightforward theft, designed to enrich landowners (denounced as "titled felons") at the expense of consumers. Repealing the law, the League held, would lower the cost of living, thus allowing employers to pay lower wages. It would also encourage Britain's trade partners to cut their own tariffs, encouraging the export of British manufactures. For these reasons, manufacturers like Richard Cobden and John Bright were at the forefront of the movement.

On the other side, landowners and farmers feared that, without price supports, British agriculture would be devastated. More fundamentally, they sensed that the Corn Laws had become an emblem of Britain's traditional power arrangements. Historically, Britain was a rural, agrarian society, where social and political authority rested on the ownership of land. Repealing the Corn Laws would mean taking power away from the country squires and handing it over to the growing cities. Cobden said plainly that he represented "not the country party, but the people who live in towns, and will govern this country." On the other side, Gladstone joked, "the Farmers looked on Throne, Church and Peerage as so many different names for the really great institution of the Country, namely the Corn Laws."

The controversy came to a head at the end of 1845, during the parliamentary recess. The Conservative Party, whose backbone was the country landowners, had always been a bastion of support for the Corn Laws. But Peel, the prime minister, had gradually become convinced that the economic case for repealing them was irresistible. When news arrived from Ireland of the beginning of the potato famine, he saw an opportunity to get rid of the Corn Laws on unimpeachably moral grounds: cheaper grain imports would mean cheaper food for the Irish. In fact, as Peel's opponents predicted at the time, repeal did nothing to help the starving peasants of Ireland, who couldn't afford to buy grain at any price. But when Parliament convened in January 1846, Peel was determined to have his way; and while his followers were unhappy, his personal authority was so great that it looked as though no one would be able to stop him.

Disraeli, however, saw that his opportunity to bring Peel down had finally arrived. For the last several years, his attacks on the prime minister over various issues had grown sharper and sharper. On each occasion, the substance of Disraeli's criticism was that Peel's Conservatism was purely pragmatic, that there was no principle he could be trusted to uphold. "I never knew the right honourable gentleman [to] bring forward" a proposal, Disraeli mocked in an 1845 speech, "without saying that three courses were open to us. In a certain sense, and looking to his own position, he is right. There is the course the right honourable gentleman has left. There is the course the right honourable gentleman is following; and there is usually the course the right honourable gentleman ought to follow."

Now, by changing his mind about the Corn Laws, Peel had abandoned the most important plank in the Conservative platform. Many Tory MPs feared that they would be direct financial losers from repeal, since their estates would produce less rent. Even more important, however, they resented the way Peel expected them to abandon their political pledges. The MPs of Disraeli's day, it is important to remember, were seldom professional politicians, elected by their party's efforts and expected to toe the party line. Especially in the Tory Party, they were usually men of authority in their counties—landowners, magistrates, and large employers, accustomed to deference. "Right or wrong," as Disraeli described them, "they were men of honour, breeding, and refinement, high and generous character, weight and station in the country." They were not used to the kind of high-handed treatment they received from Peel.

The root of their disaffection was made very clear by

Lord George Bentinck, a previously undistinguished Tory MP who now became Peel's most vocal opponent. The prime minister had "insulted the honour of parliament and of the country," he declared, "and it is now time that atonement should be made to the betrayed constituencies of the empire." Still more bluntly, Bentinck said: "I keep horses in three counties, and they tell me that I shall save fifteen hundred a year by free trade. I don't care for that; what I cannot bear is being *sold*." If there was one thing Disraeli understood, it was this conception of honor. He considered himself a born aristocrat; now he determined to use his knowledge of aristocratic psychology, honed by years of observation, to rally the Conservatives against Peel.

In a series of speeches in the winter and spring of 1846, Disraeli hammered home three complementary messages. The first was that Peel was an unprincipled opportunist. "My idea of a great statesman is of one who represents a great idea," Disraeli said, whereas Peel "is no more a great statesman than the man who gets up behind a carriage is a great whip." (Later, he compared Peel's treatment of the Corn Laws to that of a nurse entrusted with a baby who "dashes its brains out.") Second, Disraeli reminded the Tories that they had given their word of honor to support the Corn Laws: "Let men stand by the principle by which they rise, right or wrong." Finally, he insisted, as he had since the beginning of his career, that the landed aristocracy were England's natural leaders. "You value that territorial constitution, not as serving to gratify the pride or pamper the luxury of the proprietors of the land," he argued, "but because in that constitution you . . . have found the only security for self-government."

But it was Disraeli's tone, as much as his arguments, that made his attacks on Peel so effective. Peel was known for his arrogant demeanor. "The fact is," he once said, "people like a certain degree of obstinacy and presumption in a Minister." After five years as prime minister, he had rubbed many of his supporters the wrong way. They were delighted, then, to see Disraeli goad him past endurance. *Fraser's Magazine* described Disraeli's "peculiar" debating style:

> he seems so careless, supercilious, indifferent to the trouble of pleasing. . . . His words are not so much delivered as that they flow from the mouth, as if it were really too much trouble for so clever, so intellectual—in a word, so literary a man to speak at all. . . . In conveying an innuendo, an ironical sneer, or a suggestion of contempt, which courtesy forbids him to translate into words—in conveying such masked enmities by means of a glance, a shrug, an altered tone of voice, or a transient expression of face, he is unrivalled.

Disraeli's campaign reached its climax on May 15, when he delivered a three-hour philippic against Peel, calling him "a burglar of others' intellect," charging him with "political petty larceny," and concluding with a resounding appeal to "the cause of labour, the cause of the people, the cause of England!" Inevitably, the battle was lost. It had been clear from the beginning that the support of the Whigs, along with the moderate Tories who came to be called Peelites, would be enough to repeal the Corn Laws. But Disraeli and Bentinck had won the war, damaging Peel so severely that he could no longer remain head of the Conservative Party. A month later, when a bill regarding police measures in Ireland came up for a vote, the bulk of the Conservatives—now calling themselves Protectionists—joined the Whigs in voting against it, and Peel was forced to resign. He had managed to get rid of the Corn Laws, but only at the price of his own career. He died in 1850 without ever returning to office.

The fall of Peel made Disraeli's subsequent rise possible. But it was also an example of the way all his triumphs turned out to be ambiguous ones. Like *Vivian Grey*, like his campaigns at High Wycombe, the battle with Peel made Disraeli notorious rather than popular. At the time he was driven from office, the prime minister was well liked in the country at large, certainly much more so than the man who defeated him. Even Isaac D'Israeli told his son that Peel "seems a good sort of man, and the only popular one in the country." It didn't help matters that, during one debate, Peel referred to Disraeli's begging him for office in 1841. Instead of a principled dissenter, Disraeli could be seen as a mere disappointed office-seeker, and it is surely true that, had he been a member of Peel's government, he would never have launched his righteous crusade.

The mixed feelings that Disraeli's feat inspired can be seen clearly in a letter he received from the Tory Lord Ponsonby. He complimented Disraeli's skill, saying that he was "born to the foremost rank of [England's] chiefest ornaments and leaders." But the exact wording of his compliment was bound to make Disraeli ponder: "I doubt if any classic orator of Rome or England ever did anything so well as you crucified Peel. Had I been him, I would have rushed at and murdered you, or run home and hanged myself." The best-known Jew in England had "crucified" England's beloved leader: it was an uncomfortable echo of the deicidal language that had once made Disraeli challenge O'Connell. And many people shared the sense that what Disraeli had accomplished, while impressive, was not honorable—not something that a true Englishman could or would have done. One of the leading Peelites described Disraeli as "the Red Indian of debate. By the use of the tomahawk he has cut his way to power." Queen Victoria said that the House of Commons should be "ashamed" of having "that detestable Mr. D'Israeli" in its ranks. Even the Earl of Derby, who succeeded Peel as head of the Conservative Party, had to acknowledge the "jealousy and hatred (the word is not too strong) felt by the Peelite party in the House of Commons towards Disraeli."

Disraeli's reputation was, in fact, a large part of the reason why the Conservatives remained out of power for most of the next twenty years. When Peel left the Protectionists, who in time reclaimed the name of Conservatives, the members of his government went with him. Almost all the Tories with official experience, including Gladstone, were now Peelites, sitting as an independent faction in Parliament. And as long as Disraeli was at the head of the Conservatives, the Peelites would never agree to reunite with them. On several occasions, Disraeli even offered to resign his leadership position if it would coax Gladstone and other influential men back into the fold; but the bitterness went too deep. For the next two decades, an alliance of Whigs and Peelites ran the country, leaving the Conservatives in permanent opposition. Only when the governing coalition was briefly split, by personal or political tensions, could the Conservatives form a weak, temporary government. Disraeli's rebellion against Peel had put him on the front bench at last, but the prospect of his ever becoming prime minister still seemed remote.

12

From 1846 until his retirement in 1868, the Earl of Derby led the Conservative Party from the House of Lords. In the House of Commons, however, the only men of talent or recognized authority were Bentinck and Disraeli; and Bentinck, who had previously devoted all his energies to horse-racing, was an awkward, unenthusiastic leader. As it turned out, Disraeli was to take his place almost immediately, and by the strangest of means. Not even in a novel could Disraeli have imagined that the Jewish question would end up making a Jew the leader of the most anti-Jewish faction in Parliament.

The condition of the Jews in England, by the mid-nineteenth century, was possibly the best of any country in Europe. Members of elite Jewish families were even beginning to win honored places in English society: in the 1830s, Moses Montefiore was the first Jew to be elected Sheriff of London, and F. H. Goldsmid became the first Jew admitted to the Bar. But it was still impossible for a believing Jew to become a Member of Parliament. This was not due to a deliberate anti-Jewish policy, but the unforeseen result of an old technicality. During the reign of William III, an "oath of abjuration" was imposed on MPs, requiring them to deny any allegiance to the deposed Stuart dynasty. By Disraeli's day, the Stuarts were ancient history, but the oath was still legally required—including the phrase "upon the true faith of a Christian," which made it impossible for practicing Jews to take it. The Jewish community began to agitate for a change in the wording of the oath around the time of the Catholic emancipation debate, in the late 1820s. The first bill to that effect was introduced, and rejected, in 1830. Three further attempts were made in the 1830s, and each time the legislation was thrown out by the House of Lords.

So far, however, the question of admitting Jews to Parliament was strictly hypothetical. The only MPs of Jewish origin were professing Christians, who had no problem taking the oath—including David Ricardo, the economist, and Disraeli himself. But in 1847, in the first election after the fall of Peel, Lionel de Rothschild was elected to Parliament for the City of London. Now the Jewish question became a practical one, on which every politician had to take a stand. For the Liberals, as the Whigs and their Radical allies were now being called, this presented no difficulty. Since 1688, the Whigs had been the party of religious liberty; Rothschild had been elected as a Liberal; and most English Jews voted for the Liberals.

In December 1847, then, the new Whig prime minister, Lord John Russell, introduced a bill to exempt Jews from taking the oath "upon the true faith of a Christian." There was a clear majority for the bill in the House of Commons. After all, both Protestant Dissenters and Roman Catholics were already allowed in Parliament, and those groups were much larger, and historically more antagonistic to the Church of England, than the Jews. Most MPs agreed with Gladstone that "the admission of an extremely small fraction of Jews into Parliament" could hardly "paralyse and nullify the Christianity of all those who sit there."

But in the Conservative Party, it was another story. The Conservatives were the most tradition-bound faction in Parliament, and the most identified with the Church of England. Tory peers in the House of Lords could ensure that Jewish emancipation would never become law. Even in the Commons, the rank-and-file Tories felt that admitting Rothschild to Parliament would be an implicit admission that England was no longer a Christian country. Shaftesbury, whose solicitude for the Jews was restricted to Palestine, warned that if they opened the doors to a Jew, they would one day "have to stand out for a white Parliament; and perhaps they would have a final struggle for a male Parliament."

The emancipation debate, then, faced Disraeli with an exquisitely uncomfortable problem. He had been a leader of the Conservative Party for less than a year, and his own followers still viewed him with suspicion. If he voted against the bulk of the party, and on a Jewish issue, it would only remind them how anomalous it was that they were being led by a Jewish "adventurer." But the alternative, voting against Jewish emancipation, was unthinkable. Disraeli's political principles and his personal dignity alike demanded that he support the claims of the Jews, on which he had just expounded so vehemently in *Tancred*.

Disraeli could have made things easier for himself by casting his vote without making a speech. But he was determined to explain the reasons why he supported Jewish emancipation. "I cannot sit in this House with any misconception of my opinion on the subject," he insisted. In particular, he wanted it to be clear that he was not motivated by a belief that all men should enjoy freedom of religion. This was the standard Liberal reason for supporting the Jewish claim, and in an ever more democratic age it was a persuasive one. The Dissenters and the Catholics had been enfranchised, the middle class had been enfranchised—why not the Jews? The historian Macaulay argued along these lines in an influential essay: "Why a man should be less fit to exercise . . . power because he wears a beard, because he does not eat ham, because he goes to the synagogue on Saturdays instead of going to the church on Sundays, we cannot conceive."

Disraeli, however, had never been in sympathy with this sort of reasoning, whose premise was that all men are entitled to an equal share in government. On the contrary, his brand of Toryism was based on the notion that power should be the prerogative of the aristocracy, which was bound in turn to use its prerogatives for the common good. If Disraeli could not argue for admitting the Jews to Parliament on the basis of their natural rights, then, he had to find another compelling reason. The one he chose was theological and followed the general lines he had already laid down in *Tancred*. The Jews, he argued, deserved the respect of Christians because Jews were the inventors of Christianity.

In his novel, Disraeli had written that "Christianity is

Judaism for the multitude." Now he returned to this theme, suggesting that the difference between the two faiths was negligible. Once again, he was playing the ungrateful role of the "blank page" between the Old Testament and the New, trying to bridge what most people considered an eternal divide.

"The very reason for admitting the Jews is because they can show so near an affinity to you," he harangued. "Where is your Christianity if you do not believe in their Judaism?" He even repeated Sidonia's argument that the founders of Christianity were "only Hebrews": "All the early Christians were Jews. The Christian religion was first preached by men who had been Jews until they were converted; every man in the early ages of the Church by whose power, or zeal, or genius, the Christian faith was propagated, was a Jew." By this logic, excluding the Jews from Parliament would be a blasphemy against Jesus himself. "I will not take upon me," Disraeli melodramatically concluded, "the awful responsi-bility of excluding from the legislature those who are of the religion in the bosom of which my Lord and Saviour was born."

From one point of view, this speech of Disraeli's was a rhetorical masterpiece. So far, the debate had been framed in terms of Parliament considering whether to grant a favor to the Jews. In Disraeli's view, however, the positions were reversed. It was the Jews who had long ago bestowed a boon on England, by inventing the religion that Englishmen pro-fess; without "the genius of Judaism," there would be no

Christianity. Admitting the Jews to Parliament, then, was not granting a favor but repaying a debt. "If you had not forgotten what you owe to this people," he lectured the House, "you as Christians would be only too ready to seize the first opportunity of meeting the claims of those who profess this religion." Once again, Disraeli's aristocratic pride had led him to transform Jewishness, in his imagination, from an inferior condition to a superior one.

The House of Commons, however, did not share Disraeli's premises, and so it could not accept his conclusions. For most MPs, what mattered about Christianity was not what it had in common with Judaism but the ways it differed. They could not accept the notion that English Christians were just belated or imitation Jews. Pragmatically, then, Disraeli's intervention was a serious mistake, reminding the whole House that, on questions of religion as on other matters, he was not sound. His speech was frequently interrupted by groans, and there was no applause when he sat down. The Tory *Morning Herald* editorialized: "Theology, Mr. Disraeli, is not your vocation. The 'oh, oh's,' and 'loud laughter' of Thursday, in the House of Commons, conveyed the exact impression which your sermon has produced upon the minds of every Christian reader in the land." The Conservatives were appalled, with one MP demanding: "Must I . . . cheer Disraeli when he declares that there is no difference between those who crucified Christ and those who kneel before Christ crucified?"

Disraeli recognized that he could not win the Conservatives over to his views, and in future he kept quiet on the subject. "If I thought that anything which I could say would have tended to accomplish an object dear to my heart as to my convictions," he said, he would have continued to make speeches in favor of Jewish emancipation. "But, inasmuch as I believe that my opinions upon the subject are not shared by one single member on either side of the House," he would restrict himself to casting a silent vote. He would have many occasions to bite his tongue. Already in 1847, a majority in the Commons was willing to repeal the Jewish disabilities. But the Lords remained obstinate, and Lionel de Rothschild was unable to take his seat. He was elected again in 1849 and 1852, and each time the oath kept him out of office.

Not until 1858, after Rothschild was elected yet again, did Parliament manage to reach a typically English compromise. Each House would be allowed to draw up its own oath, so that the Commons could admit their actual Jewish member, while the Lords could retain their hypothetical ban. Lionel de Rothschild took his seat, kept it for the next sixteen years, and never made a single speech: he had made his point. In time even the Lords stopped caring about the issue, and in 1885, when Lionel's son Nathaniel became the first Jewish peer, he took his seat in the upper House without demur. As always happens, a prejudice began to seem absurd the moment it was overcome.

In 1847, however, the fallout from the Jewish debate was significant. Logically, the main victim of Conservative resentment should have been Disraeli. A party that voted against Jewish emancipation might well have bridled at being led by a Jew, and one with such strange religious opinions. But Lord George Bentinck also voted for emancipation, and as it turned out, he took the brunt of the Tory backlash. After all, the Conservatives could hardly expect Disraeli to vote otherwise than he did. They were even ready to acknowledge his courage in standing up for his fellow Jews: a few years later, a Conservative MP praised "the manly and honourable way in which [Disraeli] has come forward in support of the Jewish race." Once again, Disraeli had demonstrated Daniel Deronda's rule: there was less shame in being a Jew than it trying to deny it.

Bentinck, however, had no such excuse. He voted for Jewish emancipation out of principle, but he frankly admitted that he thought the whole question a waste of time. "I have always, I believe, voted in favour of the Jews," he wrote. "I say I believe, because I never could work myself up into caring two straws about the question one way or the other, and scarcely know how I may have voted." There were so few Jews in Britain, and so few of those were ever likely to run for Parliament, that Bentinck viewed the debate only in relation to Lionel de Rothschild's individual claims: "The Jew question I look upon as a personal matter, as I would a great private estate or Divorce Bill."

Yet Bentinck, too, took the polarizing step of making a speech on the subject, thus drawing his followers' attention to his unpopular vote. He had two reasons for doing so. First, he was disgusted by the prejudices of the Conservatives: "A party that can muster 140 on a Jew Bill, and cannot muster much above half those numbers on any question essentially connected with the great interests of the empire, can only be led by their antipathies, their hatreds, and their prejudices." And second, after their joint struggle against Peel, he was unwilling to hang Disraeli out to dry. "I don't like letting Disraeli vote by himself apart from the party; otherwise I might give in to the prejudices of the multitude," he wrote. It was another proof of how seriously Bentinck took the principle of honor.

The result was deeply ironic. The arch-Protestant wing of the Tory Party rebelled against Bentinck's leadership. "We abandoned the minister who insisted upon measures which we deemed inimical to the state," wrote the *Morning Herald*, referring to Peel. "Can we stand by the leader who takes his place, and who calls for legislation which, as Christian men, we conceive hateful to GOD?" Bentinck, who had never enjoyed his leadership position, seized the opportunity to resign. But in his absence, there was no one to lead the Tories in the Commons except Disraeli; not a single member could rival his parliamentary skill and oratorical ability. The party had no choice but to elevate the one man whose views on the Jewish question were even more obnoxious than Bentinck's.

The Tories tried to get by during 1848 without a formal leader. Then, after Bentinck's sudden death in September, they patched together a leadership committee, in which Disraeli was joined by two more respectable MPs. But the arrangement was obviously a formality, and after a few years it was forgotten. Effectively until 1851, and then officially, Disraeli was the leader of the Conservatives in the House of Commons. It was a position he once despaired of ever achieving, and only a fortuitous combination of political divisions, personal enmities, and untimely deaths allowed him to claim it. As one politician observed, Disraeli was "absolutely alone, the only piece upon the board on that side of politics that was above the level of a pawn. . . . He was like a subaltern in a great battle where every superior officer was killed or wounded."

13

Disraeli's elevation to the party leadership coincided with important changes in his personal life. In April 1847, his mother died, and his father followed her in January 1848. Although they had never converted to Christianity, they were buried in the churchyard of Bradenham, where they had lived for the past twenty years. Disraeli said nothing about the first loss, in keeping with his usual silence where his mother was concerned. But the death of Isaac prompted him to edit a new edition of his father's works, and to write a memorial essay about his life. He lovingly evoked his father's character, so different from his own: "The philosophic sweetness of his disposition, the serenity of his lot, and the elevating nature of his pursuits, combined to enable him to pass through life without an evil act, almost without an evil thought." Disraeli knew that no one would pay him the same compliment. Nowhere was his difference from his father clearer than in the way he cast off the "serenity" of literary life for the strife of politics. By the same token, however, Disraeli never had to reproach himself with what he called "one of [Isaac's] few infirmities . . . a deficiency of self-esteem." His own thinking about Judaism had been largely determined by his need to fashion a self-assertive Jewish identity, in place of Isaac's self-effacing plea for "amalgamation."

Isaac's death meant that Disraeli, the eldest son, came into a substantial inheritance. It was not enough to pay off his debts—which had already consumed a large part of Mary Anne's income—but it provided timely assistance in a major project already under way: his purchase of a country estate. With Isaac gone, Disraeli would no longer have Bradenham as a retreat and base of operations in Bucking-hamshire. More important, a leader of the Conservative Party, traditionally composed of country gentlemen, needed to be a gentleman himself, and only owning land could guar-antee that status. For a politician who had just made his name defending the "territorial constitution" of England, it seemed especially strange that Disraeli had no territorial roots.

In the election of 1847, he began to remedy this situation, exchanging his Shrewsbury seat for a new one representing the county of Buckinghamshire. The boroughs, more urban and more corrupt, were the Whigs' natural constituencies; the counties, where elections were cheaper and more digni-fied, were the Tories' home ground, and winning a county seat helped to consolidate Disraeli's standing in his party. Years later, he wrote that being elected MP for his county was "the event in my public life, which has given me the greatest satisfaction." For the first time, he belonged to the class he had always praised.

That transformation was completed late in 1848, when

Disraeli purchased Hughenden, an estate in the neighborhood of High Wycombe. But the way Disraeli managed the purchase shows how tenuous his new status remained. Much too deeply in debt to be able to afford the house and grounds, he turned for help to Lord George Bentinck, and then, after his unexpected death, to Bentinck's brothers. They agreed to advance him £25,000 to complete the purchase, on the understanding that they were making an investment in Disraeli's political career, and therefore in the future of the Conservative Party. Disraeli told the Bentincks plainly "that it would be no object to them and no pleasure to me, unless I played the high game in public life; and that I could not do that without being on a rock."

He could never pay them back financially, and years later, when the Bentincks called in their loan, he had to find another Conservative benefactor to take their place. But he expressed his gratitude in a more lasting way by writing *Lord George Bentinck: A Political Biography*, which appeared in 1851. Not a true biography, the book is really Disraeli's firsthand account of the campaign to unseat Peel, designed to emphasize Bentinck's role and underplay his own. For a reader interested in the subject, it is one of Disraeli's most enjoyable books, capturing the human drama of politics in a way that few politicians' memoirs ever achieve. It also summarizes, in a chapter-length digression, the theological and racial interpretation of Judaism that Disraeli had advanced during the emancipation debate.

Even now that Disraeli owned land, however, he was not a

true country gentleman, with all the tastes and prejudices that title entailed. Hughenden was his ticket to the "high game," and while he loved spending time there, the pleasures of farming and hunting never came close, in his mind, to the allure of politics. This marked Disraeli out from many of his fellow Tories, who fled London with alacrity whenever there was a horse race or a hunt in prospect. To Lord Stanley, Disraeli "complained loudly of the apathy of the party: they could not be got to attend to business while the hunting season lasted. . . . They had good natural ability, he said, taking them as a body: but wanted culture: they never read: their leisure was passed in field sports."

Conversely, Disraeli's own attempts to impersonate a countryman came off as strained and unconvincing. Constance Rothschild noted ironically "how he tried to act up to the character he had imposed upon himself, that of the country gentleman! For dressed in his velveteen coat, his leather leggings, his soft felt hat, and carrying his little hatchet, for relieving the bark of trees from the encroaching ivy, in one of those white hands, which probably hitherto had never held anything heavier than a pen, Mr Disraeli was *the Squire.*" Certainly his neighbors were very slow to accept Disraeli as "the Squire." He found that it was easier to become a cabinet minister than to become respectable in the provinces, among the sort of proud families who move like little kings through the novels of Jane Austen. In 1858, when he was chancellor of the exchequer for the second time, he was delighted when a country neighbor came begging him for patronage. "For the Tyrwhitt Drakes to ask a service from me," he gloated, "is the Hapsburgs soliciting something from a parvenu Napoleon. After thirty years of scorn and sullenness they have melted before time and events."

The gulf between Disraeli and the natural-born gentlemen of his party had to do with more than just lifestyle. It also had important consequences for political strategy. Disraeli was never satisfied with reaching the front bench of the Opposition. He had dreamed of power ever since *Vivian Grey*, and now that it was so close, he would not rest until he tasted it. His restless ambition meant that Disraeli almost always urged an aggressive strategy in Parliament, hoping to split the Whig-Peelite coalition and form a Conservative government. His attitude is captured in a letter he wrote to a friend in 1851: "We shall certainly try to knock up the Government again, if only for the fun of the thing." But Derby, his chief, had a very different approach. To be the Earl of Derby was already to be a great man, and while he was a lifelong politician, he did not share Disraeli's need to be validated by holding office. He was usually content to remain in opposition, especially if the government pursued a moderate line. And since he was far more popular and influential than his lieutenant, Derby's policy of patience prevailed.

As a result, Disraeli spent the prime of his career, from 1847 to 1866, in almost permanent Opposition. He observed and commented on the major events of these years—the Crimean War, the Indian Mutiny, the American Civil War—but he played no real role in them. His tactical maneuvers as an opposition leader form an important chapter in British political history, but they can be briefly summarized here. From the very beginning, Disraeli's goal was to restore the Protectionist Party, mistrusted by all as a die-hard, reactionary faction, to the mainstream of political debate. First of all, this meant convincing the party to abandon its opposition to free trade, which quickly became a sacred cow of Victorian politics. This was a tricky business, since Disraeli's whole case against Peel had been based on the latter's abandonment of his protectionist principles. Disraeli's pragmatic recognition that the Corn Laws were dead—"not only dead but damned," as he put it—seemed to justify the charge that he had never cared about them at all, but merely used the issue for his personal advantage.

Such suspicions would never completely disappear. To the very end of his life, Disraeli was regarded by his foes, and sometimes by his friends, as essentially an opportunist. Lord Stanley admired Disraeli, but even he confided to his diary, "it cannot be pretended that [Disraeli] is attached to any political principles as such, or that his objects are disinterested and patriotic." Trollope made the same charge publicly in his novel *Phineas Redux*, where Disraeli—thinly disguised as Mr. Daubeny—is compared to a Renaissance condottiere: "As used to be the case with Italian Powers, [the Tories] entrusted their cause to mercenary foreign generals, soldiers of fortune, who carried their good swords whither they were wanted."

No reader of Disraeli's novels could deny that there is

some truth to this characterization. Disraeli was not the rare kind of politician who enters politics disinterestedly, for the sake of advancing a cherished cause. He did have principles—his romantic conservatism, inflected by a sincere concern for the poor, was remarkably consistent from his first campaign to his last. But he frankly acknowledged that the engine of his career was a desire for glory. As he told his constituents in an 1844 speech: "There is no doubt, gentlemen, that all men who offer themselves as candidates for public favor have motives of some sort. I candidly acknowledge that I have, and I will tell you what they are: I love fame; I love public reputation; I love to live in the eyes of the country."

Yet as Disraeli pointed out, all successful politicians have similar motives; otherwise they wouldn't become politicians. Even Gladstone, who was able to convince himself that everything he did was dictated purely by conscience, could not blind others to the fact that his conscience was oddly adept at making him prime minister. Why, then, was it only Disraeli who was saddled with the reputation of adventurer? Partly, it was an inevitable result of the position of the Tories in mid-Victorian politics. Sailing against the current of a triumphant liberalism, any Conservative leader would have been forced to throw some cherished prejudices overboard. It happened to Peel when he turned against protection, and it happened to Disraeli when he took Peel's place. "I had . . . to educate our party," he explained in an 1867 speech, but that sort of education in practicalities looked to some Tories like mere cynicism.

Underneath all the political reasons, however, it was the unavoidable fact of his Jewishness that made Disraeli's ambition suspect. A Derby or a Russell did not need to cloak his desire for power in the garments of altruism. For wealthy English aristocrats, playing the "high game" of politics was as natural as going to Eton and Oxford, or as farming and hunting: it was part of their birthright. But Disraeli, who did not go to those schools and did not enjoy those rural pursuits, was not only not an aristocrat. In the eyes of many, and perhaps in his own, he was not even English. By entering politics, he was usurping prerogatives that did not belong to him—just as, at Hughenden, he put on a gentlemanly costume that never quite fit.

Only this logic can explain why Disraeli continued to face such intense resistance, even after decades of loyal service to his country. In 1868, when he became prime minister for the first time, he had been in Parliament for over thirty years, and a party leader for twenty; yet Lady Palmerston could still complain, "We are all dreadfully disgusted at the prospect of having a Jew for our Prime Minister." Even thirty years after his death, Disraeli's entry in the *Encyclopaedia Britannica* explained that "he was an Englishman in nothing but his devotion to England." Next to the great disqualification of his Jewishness, all of his personal claims to Englishness vanished.

The paradox of Disraeli's career is that, while he could never overcome the widespread sense that it was not right for him to be prime minister, he nevertheless became prime

minister. The credit for this is due first to England's principled liberalism, which made overt religious discrimination
loathsome. Disraeli himself never valued that liberalism
enough, preferring to argue for Jewish privileges rather than
defend Jewish rights; but he was nonetheless its most prominent beneficiary. Hand in hand with this principle, perhaps,
went a more instinctive English feeling for fair play. If Disraeli did what was required for success in politics, it was felt,
he deserved the rewards. This was the tone, neither
begrudging nor enthusiastic, in which Stanley granted Disraeli's claims, after lamenting his lack of principles: "Single-
ness of purpose—contempt of obloquy—energy which no
labour can exhaust . . . forms a combination rare in political
or private life, and surely deserves some degree of respect."

Though he might not have appreciated it at the time, Disraeli's decades in opposition were also indispensable to his
eventual triumph. Only the passage of time could allow Parliament and the country to get used to Disraeli's strange
presence. As leader of the Opposition in the House of Commons, he occupied an acknowledged place in the constitutional system, and he held it for so long that he came to seem
part of the natural order of things. "The greatest compliment you can pay to a woman is to give to her your time, and
it is the same with our senate," Disraeli wrote. "A man who
is always in his place becomes a sort of favourite." He was
always in his place, so much so that his mannerisms in debate
became famous. His meticulous pronunciation; his trick of
ostentatiously looking at the clock just when an opponent's

rhetorical fury reached its climax; his habit of passing a handkerchief from hand to hand while he was delivering a speech—all these became well known in the House, and thanks to the newspapers, even outside it.

On two occasions during these years, Disraeli did manage to cross the floor of the House and sit on the government bench. In 1852, a feud between the Whig leaders led to the fall of the governing coalition. But it was only with effort that Derby and Disraeli put together a Conservative cabinet, given that all the most distinguished men in the party had left it along with Peel. The government was so full of nonentities that when the aged Duke of Wellington was told their names, he kept asking "Who?"—thus bestowing on it the inglorious nickname of the "Who? Who?" Ministry. Disraeli was made chancellor of the exchequer, responsible for preparing the budget, even though he had no financial experience (and his own finances hardly testified in his favor). When he hesitated, Derby reassured him that "they give you the figures"—a nice example of the amateur spirit in which the government of an empire could still be conducted.

After fifteen years in Parliament, Disraeli was in office at last, and he relished the moment. As he told one colleague, he "felt just like a young girl going to her first ball." But the Conservative government never had a majority in the House, and it could be ejected anytime the Whigs and Peelites decided to make the effort. In December, when Disraeli presented his first full budget, Gladstone tore it to pieces, calling it "the most subversive in its tendencies . . . that I have ever known"; the House voted against it, and the government was forced to resign. Disraeli's first term of office had lasted just ten months. To add insult to injury, Gladstone replaced him at the Exchequer.

He would not get another chance at power for six years. There was a moment in 1855, with the Peelite-led government in disgrace over its conduct of the Crimean War, when the Conservatives might have been able to force their way back into office. But Derby characteristically refused to press the attack, allowing the conservative Whig Lord Palmerston to become prime minister instead. Palmerston prosecuted the war vigorously and became immensely popular, remaining in power, with one break, for the next ten years. Disraeli was furious, feeling that Derby had let the party down from sheer lack of willpower. "I have never yet been fairly backed in life," he had complained the year before. "All the great persons I have known, even when what is called 'ambitious' by courtesy, have been unequal to a grand game." Once again, events conspired to teach Disraeli the virtue most foreign to his nature: patience.

He would get the chance to return to the Exchequer in February 1858, when Palmerston's government fell after a diplomatic imbroglio with France. Once again the Conservatives took power as a minority government, and once again their tenure lasted less than a year. This time the defeat came on a new reform bill, the Conservatives' attempt to take the lead in what was shaping up to be an inevitable second round of electoral reform. The Liberals united to defeat the bill, but the issue of reform was not dead. In Derby's third government, the difficulty of broadening the franchise while still remaining true to Conservative principles would present Disraeli with the biggest challenge of his career.

Even if Disraeli was not in office long enough to make any real changes in policy, he still enjoyed the glory of being a minister. By now, he also had an unlikely new friend to share the triumph with. In 1851, Disraeli received a letter out of the blue from a Mrs. Brydges Willyams, a colonel's widow, who offered to make him the heir to her fortune. The reason for this largesse, it transpired, was that Mrs. Brydges Willyams was born Sarah Mendez da Costa, a Sephardic Jew, and she saw in Disraeli a champion of the Jewish people. After some deliberation Disraeli accepted the offer, and when his benefactress died, in 1863, he inherited £30,000. In exchange for her bequest, she asked only to be buried at Hughenden, in the graveyard where Disraeli and Mary Anne would also lie.

But in the interim, Mrs. Brydges Willyams's friendship was an even more important gift, and she became one of Disraeli's best correspondents. It is clear that he viewed his new friend, who was close to eighty when they first met, as a kind of surrogate mother, the latest in a long line of adoring older women. When he returned to office in 1858, she was one of the first people he notified; when he left the next year, she received his last letter on official stationery.

Disraeli's letters to Mrs. Brydges Willyams were often taken up with flowery compliments and advice on health problems. ("Something taken half an hour before repose, very nutritious but very light, might charm your eyelids," he suggests.) But it also reveals a side of Disraeli's personality that he kept hidden from his colleagues. Most obviously, his new friend could enter into Disraeli's speculations about Jews and Jewishness in a way that even Mary Anne could not. He sent her a copy of *Tancred*, describing it as "a vindication, and, I hope, a complete one, of the race from which we alike spring." The fact that they were both converts who had married Christians allowed Disraeli to be frank with Mrs. Brydges Willyams about his ambivalence toward Judaism: "I, like you, was not bred among my race, and was nurtured in great prejudice against them," he confided. For that very reason, perhaps, they both played the game of inventing a noble genealogy for themselves, and Mrs. Brydges Willyams enlisted Disraeli in getting her "family crest" recognized by the College of Heralds. Disraeli's theories about Judaism were unpopular with almost everyone else, but Mrs. Brydges Willyams embraced them. In her will, she testified to "my approbation and admiration of his efforts to vindicate the race of Israel, with my views respecting which he is acquainted, and which I have no doubt he will endeavour to accomplish."

But perhaps Mrs. Brydges Willyams was most important to Disraeli as an audience for his triumphs. In his professional life, he remained essentially solitary, never making close friends out of the colleagues who distrusted him. Only someone outside the political world—in fact, only a Jew— could appreciate how far Disraeli had come to reach his present eminence. In subtle ways, Disraeli's letters to his benefactress, like his letters to his sister, express a certain amazement at all the things that are happening to him. He writes about a country neighbor whose estate once belonged to the Roundhead leader Hampden: "Such is history, and such is life! Strange things both," is his wondering comment. When the queen sends him "a fat buck" from her private preserve, he sends the neck on to Mrs. Brydges Willyams, knowing that she will share his delight at being included in the royal bounty.

To other squires, such proximity to history and royalty would be a matter of course; to Disraeli, they are always like something out of a fairy tale. This sense of his own sheer unlikeliness never left Disraeli, and it remains one of the most attractive things about him. As a novelist and as a Jew, he was alienated from his own experience just enough to appreciate its strangeness, but never too much to enjoy it. On the contrary, he relished his own exploits far more articulately than other politicians, precisely because he never took them for granted. He knew the ironic pleasure reserved for those who imagine a life for themselves, and then actually bring it into being. And that pleasure could only be consummated by sharing it with an adoring female audience—like Mrs. Brydges Willyams, or like Sarah, whose death in 1859 grieved him deeply. When Disraeli finally became prime minister, a friend commiserated with him: "If only your sister had been alive to witness your triumph, what happiness it would have given her." "Ah, poor Sa! poor Sa!" he replied, "we've lost our audience, we've lost our audience."

14

By 1865, Palmerston had been prime minister for a decade, with one interruption, and it seemed that he could remain in office indefinitely. But in October he died, just before his eighty-first birthday, and the Liberal Lord John Russell returned to office as prime minister. Russell had been one of the architects of the Reform Bill more than thirty years earlier, and he was now determined to complete his work by further broadening the franchise. Gladstone, who became leader of the House of Commons—Disraeli's opposite number—championed the new Reform measure, which was hardly radical in scope. The Liberals planned to lower the property qualification for voters in both counties and boroughs, adding four hundred thousand new voters to the rolls. Even after that expansion, however, only a quarter of the adult male population would have the right to vote.

The Conservative Party was not dead-set against Reform—Disraeli himself had tried to pass a Reform Bill in 1859—but it considered Russell's bill excessive. By themselves, the Tories could not have defeated it; but a section of the Liberals, too, were opposed to extending the franchise, and they rebelled against their leaders. For three months Parliament debated the bill, with Disraeli deliberately keeping in the background and allowing the dissident Liberals to lead the attack. Finally, in June 1866, the bill was defeated, when nearly fifty Liberals joined the Conservatives in opposition. Russell's government resigned, and Derby and Disraeli were back in office for a third time.

Once again, the Tories were in a precarious situation, governing without a majority in the Commons. But this time Disraeli saw a way to extend their tenure, by taking up the complex and increasingly urgent question of Reform. A month after Russell's bill was defeated, pro-Reform demonstrators assembled for a meeting in London's Hyde Park. When the police denied them permission to enter the park, a crowd of several thousand broke down the railings and rioted for three days. The disturbance was comparatively minor—nothing like the near-revolutionary conditions of 1832—but it helped fuel the government's belief that some measure of Reform had to be achieved.

The Reform question placed Disraeli in a difficult position, since it represented a collision of the two principles that had always guided his political career. In theory, he was opposed to broadening the franchise, believing that political power was rightly lodged in England's propertied classes. Back in 1835, when he was writing articles against Reform for the Tory press, he held that the idea that pure democracy "could be established in this ancient realm is morally and physically impossible." During the debate over Russell's bill, he continued to make the same point: "I think that this House should remain a House of Commons, and not become a House of the People, a House of a mere indiscriminate multitude." Universal suffrage might work in America, he believed, but in England it would result in disaster.

Yet at the same time, Disraeli had also raised pragmatism to the level of a principle. Ever since the fall of Peel, he had struggled to "educate his party," to rid the Tories of obsolete shibboleths and make them a viable electoral prospect. He recognized that politics is the art of the possible, and he believed that an obstinate anti-Reform position was impossible in the liberal climate of the day. By embracing Reform, on the other hand, Disraeli could once again make the Conservatives a constructive political force. Nor would he have been ashamed to admit that personal ambition played a role in his decision making. If the Conservatives passed Reform, they might finally win an election, and Disraeli could become something more than the second in command of a caretaker government.

The challenge for Disraeli, then, was to frame a Reform Bill that would be liberal enough to satisfy the public, yet somehow conservative enough to convince his own followers. He tried to square this circle by introducing the principle of plural voting. Every male head of a household would get the vote, under Disraeli's initial plan, but those with certain qualifications—members of a high tax bracket, holders of a university degree—would get an extra vote. But these "fancy franchises," as they were mockingly called, proved very unpopular, and Disraeli was forced to drop them.

After bitter internal disagreements, which pulled the

government in every possible direction during the first months of 1867, Disraeli decided to go ahead with a bill based on simple household suffrage, without plural voting. This was an even more expansive measure than the one the Tories had originally defeated, and three members of the cabinet resigned in protest. Disraeli felt confident of the bill, however, because it rested on a technicality: only householders who paid their own rates, or property taxes, could register to vote. This would eliminate most town dwellers who rented their houses, since it was standard practice for renters to pay rates through their landlord—a practice known as "compounding." Compounders, under Disraeli's plan, would not be eligible to vote, thus disenfranchising a large swath of the urban working class.

By now, however, Disraeli had compromised on so many issues, and come so close to victory, that he could not bear to let even this crucial point stand in the way of passing a Reform Bill. When a Liberal member made a proposal to abolish compounding, Disraeli agreed, without consulting any of his colleagues. The change effectively added another five hundred thousand voters to the rolls, and turned the Conservative bill into a measure that even some Radicals believed went too far. But the Tories were intoxicated by the prospect of victory—the chance, as Disraeli put it, to "extinguish Gladstone and Co."—and they followed their leader. In August 1867, the Second Reform Bill became law, and more than a million Englishmen gained the right to vote. In the words of the historian Gertrude Himmelfarb,

"The Reform Act of 1867 was one of the decisive events, perhaps *the* decisive event, in modern English history. It was this act that transformed England into a democracy."

No one deserved more of the credit than Disraeli, and everyone knew it. To the Conservatives, he was the hero of the hour, responsible for their greatest legislative victory in twenty years. When he went to the Carlton Club after one important vote, he was met with cheers and a toast: "Here's to the man who rode the race, who took the time, who kept the time, and who did the trick." Disraeli must have especially savored a new joke that made the rounds: "Why is Gladstone like a telescope? Because Disraeli draws him out, looks through him, and shuts him up."

But at the same time, it was hard to avoid the suspicion that Disraeli had only won this Conservative triumph by abandoning Conservative principles. That, at least, was how it looked to diehards like the Marquess of Salisbury. "If it be a Conservative triumph to have adopted the principles of your most determined adversary," he wrote, "then in the whole course of your annals I will venture to say the Conservative party has won no triumph so signal as this." Salisbury accused Disraeli of turning the party into the tool of his personal ambition: "As far as I can judge the one object for which they are striving heartily is the premiership of Mr. Disraeli."

Even this might not have been so bad, Salisbury continued, if it weren't for the old problem of Disraeli's Jewishness. "If I had a firm confidence in his principles or his honesty, or even if he were identified by birth or property with the Conservative classes in the country—I might in the absence of any definite professions work to maintain him in power. But he is an adventurer: & as I have too good cause to know, he is without principles and honesty." A political feat that might have been applauded in a natural-born Tory was deeply suspect in a Jew, who, by definition, could be nothing more than an adventurer.

Salisbury was not the only critic to take this implicitly anti-Semitic line. The passage of the Reform Bill could not have had less to do with religion in general, or with Disraeli's religion in particular. But any attack on Disraeli could turn, in the hands of his enemies, into an attack on his Jewishness, as though his objectionable actions were always traceable to his "race." Sometimes this point was made explicitly, as when one Tory MP asked "how he could accept extreme Reform from a bad Jew, after having refused moderate Reform from a good Christian"; or when the poet Coventry Patmore denounced "The year of the great crime,/When the false English nobles, and their Jew,/By God demented, slew/The trust they stood twice pledged to keep from wrong." Other critics resorted to racial metaphors to capture their sense of Disraeli's foreignness: "The Ethiopian will not change his skin," Gladstone remarked.

From another point of view, however, Disraeli's Reform Bill appears as not merely a tactical maneuver but the consummation of his long-held principles. After all, he had never been the kind of reactionary who fought change at all costs. He had always been a Tory because he believed the Tories were the "national party," best equipped to address the needs of the whole community, including workers and the poor. As he said in a triumphant speech in 1867: "Whenever the Tory party degenerates into an oligarchy it becomes unpopular; whenever the national institutions do not fulfil their original intention, the Tory party becomes odious; but when the people are led by their natural leaders . . . the Tory party is triumphant." Giving the vote to the workers, then, might introduce a powerful new Conservative force into politics. The challenge in the next phase of Disraeli's career would be to convince the new voters that the Tories were better guardians of their interests than the Liberals.

Disraeli did not have to wait long to reap the reward of his victory. Early in 1868, Derby was forced by declining health to resign from office; he would die the next year. Disraeli, fresh off the Reform triumph, was his inevitable successor as leader of the Conservative Party, and thus as prime minister in the Conservative government. On February 27, he went to see Queen Victoria and was formally appointed to office. He would only be prime minister for nine months, and his party was still in the minority. When the next general election was called, in November 1868, Gladstone and the Liberals would win a crushing victory on the expanded franchise. But for a brief moment—forty-two years after *Vivian Grey*, thirty-six years after his first run for Parliament, twenty years after becoming a leader of the Conservative Party—Disraeli had reached his goal. Characteristically, he played down his triumph: "I have climbed to the top of the greasy pole," he said nonchalantly.

Disraeli's first term as Prime Minister was too brief for him to institute any major new policies, though he delighted in the chance to deal out honors and titles. As it turned out, he was in office at just the right time to appoint a new Viceroy of India and a new Archbishop of Canterbury. He also took the opportunity to claim a peerage—not for himself, since that would have meant leaving the House of Commons, but for Mary Anne, whom the queen made a Viscountess. It was Disraeli's way of paying homage to the wife who made his career possible, in more ways than one.

In fact, his term as Prime Minister, short as it was, may well have seemed to Disraeli like a fitting conclusion to his career. Certainly the novelist in him would have appreciated the symmetry: his journey from *Vivian Grey* to Downing Street was a perfect narrative arc. At the age of sixty-four, leading a party that had not won an election in almost thirty years, Disraeli probably doubted that he would ever clamber back up to the top of the greasy pole. Perhaps that is why, practically the instant he left office, Disraeli began working on a new novel—his first since *Tancred* more than twenty years earlier.

Writing was a way of earning money, and of filling his time now that he was facing an indefinite future out of power. But more important, it was a way of asserting the continuity of his life, of keeping faith with the man he had been when political power was only a dream. He was not simply a politician, Disraeli seemed to insist, but a man of imagination; his political career, in fact, could be considered a greater imaginative achievement than any of his books. The fact that novel writing meant taking a risk with his hard-won reputation was the opposite of a deterrent. "His wisest friends think that it must be a mistake, and his enemies hope that it will be his ruin," one politician commented, but Disraeli pressed on.

Certainly *Lothair*, which was published in 1870, was not written with the typical caution of the professional politician. In its way, it is as fantastic and provocative as *Tancred*, offering a defiantly eccentric take on the major issues of European politics. The hero is another one of Disraeli's young, naive noblemen. When we first meet him, Lothair, the orphaned son of rich parents, is an undergraduate at Oxford. But his political education, which forms the substance of the novel, reads like a spoof of Coningsby's or Egremont's. They at least were earnest seekers after wisdom, while Lothair is a self-satisfied, ignorant prig. When he is advised to enter society to gain "knowledge of the world," he replies, "Oh! as for that, my opinions are already formed on every subject; that is to say, every subject of importance; and, what is more, they will never change."

This certitude is soon shaken, as Lothair becomes the prize in a social and intellectual tug-of-war. On one side is the Catholic Church, in the person of the worldly and manipulative Cardinal Grandison—Disraeli's malicious portrait of Cardinal Manning, the leading Catholic prelate in England. Grandison, who decides that winning Lothair for the Church would be a propaganda coup, maneuvers him into the clutches of a rich Catholic family with a beautiful, pious daughter. He is on the brink of converting when he meets and falls in love with the mysterious Theodora—who, he soon learns, is the head of a secret society of atheist republicans, devoted to expelling the pope from Rome. Lothair follows his new muse to Italy, and he is marching on Rome with Garibaldi's revolutionary army when he is knocked unconscious in a battle. When he awakens, he finds that he has been rescued by Catholics, who have told the world that he was fighting on the pope's side, and was saved from death by an appearance of the Virgin Mary.

As even this summary shows, the plot of *Lothair* is at once silly and politically fearless. Disraeli's irreverent wit, which had always been the life of his fiction, has a plump target in the Catholic Church, and the novel luxuriates in a kind of religious camp. At the same time, however, Disraeli seems to take quite seriously the idea that the struggle between the Catholic Church and revolutionary "secret societies" is the real motive force of contemporary politics. "After all," says one character, "it is the Church against the secret societies. They are the only two strong things in Europe, and will survive kings, emperors, or parliaments."

In 1870, this might have sounded extravagant, but history

would prove it to be literally true. Fifty years later, the tsar and the kaiser were gone, while the Church and the Communists remained. Yet Disraeli's own position in this struggle is never made quite clear. As a conservative, he would naturally take the side of the Church, which represents tradition and hierarchy, against groups like the Carbonari, which fight for republicanism and national liberation. When Grandison defends the idea of theocracy, it is in much the same language Disraeli had used in *Tancred:* "There can be no political freedom which is not founded on Divine authority; otherwise it can be at the best but a specious phantom of license inevitably terminating in anarchy."

The main reason Catholicism appeals to Lothair is that it offers a refuge from the spiritual quandaries of the age, and especially from the specter of Darwinism. The publication of *The Origin of Species* in 1859 raised an unanswerable challenge to the biblical account of creation, and the problem of reconciling science and faith continued to trouble the best minds of Victorian England. Disraeli did not shy away from this debate, and all his inclinations led him to join the anti-Darwinian side. His position was not that evolution was false—it is highly unlikely that he devoted enough time to Darwin's works to form an opinion of the theory—but rather that it ought not to be true. In a speech at Oxford in 1864, Disraeli insisted that "man is a being born to believe," and that depriving him of his Christian beliefs would leave him dangerously demoralized. He summarized the evolution debate in another famous phrase. "What is the question now placed before society with a glib assurance the most astounding?" he demanded. "The question is this—Is man an ape or an angel? My Lord, I am on the side of the angels."

But there is also another "scientific" issue in *Lothair*, one more consequential for Disraeli's legacy than the debate over evolution. In the quarter-century since *Coningsby*, when Disraeli first advanced his racial theories, the pseudoscience of race had made great strides. He could not have failed to notice, however, that scientific racism had not worked to the advantage of the Jews, as he had hoped. On the contrary, it was precisely Sidonia's cherished Semitic race that figured as the villain in the new racist worldview. Gobineau, the first influential race theorist, set the tone by decrying "Semitization," the process of racial contamination that led to the decline of the Aryan peoples.

In *Lothair*, Disraeli addresses this trend through the character of Mr. Phoebus, a painter who crosses the hero's path several times. Phoebus, who is clearly a reader of Gobineau, lectures Lothair on the glories of Aryanism and the perils of Semitism. The principles of art, he insists, are "Aryan principles . . . calculated to maintain the health and beauty of a first-rate race." Conversely, the rise of "Semitism," in the form of Christianity, "destroyed art; it taught man to despise his own body." Phoebus calls for a return to the Aryan ideals of instinct, ignorance, and bodily perfection: "Books are fatal; they are the curse of the human race. . . . To render his body strong and supple is the first duty of man." The first step in the regeneration of mankind, he declares, is the elimination of Semites: "The fate of a nation will ultimately depend upon the strength and health of the population. . . . Nothing can be done until the Aryan races are extricated from Semitism."

Phoebus, in other words, sounds alarmingly like a Nazi propagandist, hymning the blond beast and strength through joy. It is as though Disraeli were making atonement, through this character, for the pernicious racial doctrines he had once so blithely advanced. Yet even now Disraeli is unable to take Phoebus, and the future he represents, entirely seriously. By the end of the novel, he has been revealed as a mere hypocrite, ready to throw his Aryanism overboard in order to benefit his career. When we last see him, he is about to go to Palestine, the homeland of Semitism and "the great Asian mystery," to make Christian paintings for the tsar. "If they would make me a Prince at once and give me the Alexander Newsky in brilliants it might be worth thinking of," he muses.

This comic turn is Disraeli's all-too-simple way of dismissing the danger Phoebus represents. Surely, he seems to be saying, no one could take Aryanism entirely seriously. Indeed, the idea that anti-Jewish prejudice was purely a medieval phenomenon, doomed to die out in the enlightened modern world, was one of Disraeli's central assumptions. In the preface to an 1849 edition of *Coningsby*, he had written that "the Jews were looked upon in the middle ages as an accursed race, the enemies of God and man"; but this hatred, what Disraeli called "the odium and stigma of medieval malevolence," could be confidently relegated to the benighted past. Writing a "General Preface" to a new edition of his works in 1870, the same year *Lothair* was published, Disraeli took it for granted that "the house of Israel [is] now freed from the barbarism of medieval misconception, and judged, like all other races, by their contributions to the existing sum of human welfare."

Disraeli did not, and possibly could not, recognize that the European "misconception" of Jews was too deeply rooted to be so easily abolished. In the years after his death, anti-Semitic prejudice would find new, unimpeachably modern forms for its "malevolence"; and the most destructive of them all would be the very pseudoscientific racism that Disraeli once looked to as a means of bolstering Jewish pride. But for Disraeli to see Phoebus as a prophet, rather than a fool, would have been too bitter an admission. It would have meant acknowledging that his lifelong attempt to bridge the Old Testament and the New was doomed—and that his own career, instead of offering new hope for European Jews, could only be regarded as a spectacular dead-end.

15

In 1872, Mary Anne Disraeli, now eighty years old, fell seriously ill with stomach cancer. After months of suffering, which she concealed as best she could, she finally succumbed on December 15. The ordeal of her sickness and death hit Disraeli extremely hard, leading him to expose the kind of emotion he almost always kept hidden. "*I am totally unable to meet the catastrophe*," he wrote to one colleague; to another he confided, in tears, "When I tell my coachman to drive home I feel it is a mockery." Condolences from the queen and a public tribute from Gladstone did nothing to console him. For thirty-four years, Mary Anne had been his closest companion and his most important audience. Now he was sixty-eight, one of the most famous men in the country, with thousands of social and professional acquaintances. Indeed, few politicians of any stripe were as socially eligible as Disraeli; fashionable hostesses would far sooner invite him to a party or a country weekend than the overearnest Gladstone. But with no children and no truly intimate friends, the death of Mary Anne left Disraeli profoundly alone. The remainder of his life, which saw his greatest political triumphs, would be shadowed by that loneliness.

One measure of the void in Disraeli's life is the alacrity

with which he tried to fill it. The summer after Mary Anne's death, he began a strange, quasi-amorous relationship with two middle-aged sisters, Selina, Countess of Bradford and Anne, Countess of Chesterfield. He had known them both since the 1830s, but he now began to court them ardently—platonically in the case of Anne, romantically with the younger, and married, Selina. Over the next eight years, he wrote the sisters a combined sixteen hundred letters—an average of one every other day, even after he returned to office in 1874. The letters to Lady Bradford, especially, sound besotted, in a way one would hardly expect from a sitting Prime Minister in his seventies: "I am certain there is no greater misfortune, than to have a heart that will not grow old. It requires all the sternness of public life to sustain one. If we have to govern a great country, we ought not to be *distrait*, and feel the restlessness of love."

He wrote Lady Bradford during sessions of Parliament and cabinet meetings, sometimes sending messengers twice a day. Like a teenager, he contrived to run into her at parties. "The other day," he wrote in 1874, "you said it was wonderful that I could write to you, with all the work and care I have to encounter. It is because my feelings impel me to write to you. It was my duty and my delight: the duty of my heart and the delight of my life. I do not think I was very unreasonable. I have never asked anything from you but your society." Clearly, what Disraeli wanted was not a sexual relationship, but the kind of affection and attention he had once received from Mary Anne. As he had told her so many years before, "My nature demands that my life should be perpetual love." Even when Selina made it clear that his attentions were burdensome, Disraeli could not help sounding needy. "I could not contemplate life without seeing you every day," he pleaded. No passage of his public or private life reveals him in a more moving light than this late, one-sided love affair.

He also dealt with his grief in a more productive way, by plunging back into politics. After the election of 1868, Disraeli had returned to his old post of leader of the Opposition, but he had been less active in Parliament than usual, recognizing that the Liberal majority was unbeatable. But the year of Mary Anne's death saw several important shifts in the political landscape. In February 1872, a service was held at St. Paul's Cathedral to give thanks for the Prince of Wales's recovery from an illness. All the leading politicians attended, passing through a large crowd on their way into the church. Gladstone, the prime minister, was booed by the spectators, while Disraeli was met with loud cheers and applause. It was a sign that the country was growing tired of the Liberal government but also that Disraeli had outlived his bad reputation. He had been in politics for so long that he was now accepted as part of the establishment, and even regarded with affection.

Later in the year, Disraeli capitalized on this momentum with two major policy speeches. He seldom spoke to large crowds, preferring to use his powers in debate. But at a mass meeting in Manchester in April, and then at London's Crystal Palace in June, he set forth two themes that would be crucial to the future of the Conservative Party. First, he committed to improving the living standards of the poor, which decades of laissez-faire Liberal government had done little to raise. Ever since writing *Sybil* in 1845, Disraeli had felt that the Tories had a particular obligation to remedy the evils that the Industrial Revolution brought to the working class. Now he promised to address "the state of the dwellings of the people, the moral consequences of which are not less considerable than the physical," as well as "the regulation of their industry, the inspection of their toil . . . [and] the purity of their provisions." He found a motto for this health-and-welfare policy in a pun on the biblical phrase "Vanity of vanities, all is vanity": "*Sanitas sanitatum, omnia sanitas.*"

At the same time, Disraeli moved to associate the Conservative Party with the cause of the Empire. The Liberals were never very enthusiastic about Britain's colonies, seeing them as a drain on the budget and an obstacle to free trade—though they never tried to get rid of them, either. Now Disraeli warned that the Liberals were out "to effect the disintegration of the Empire of England." He proceeded to gloss over the odious reality of colonialism with the abstract poetry of Empire. The choice facing the electorate, he claimed, was "whether you will be content to be a comfortable England, modelled and moulded upon Continental principles and meeting in due course an inevitable fate, or whether you will be a great country, an Imperial country, a country where your sons, when they rise, rise to paramount positions, and obtain not merely the esteem of their countrymen, but command the respect of the world."

It was Disraeli's clearest statement yet of his romantic vision of the Israel of his imagination. While rhetoric about national unity and glory had always been his stock-in-trade, however, he had never had the chance, or the obligation, to translate it into actual policy. But in early 1874, Gladstone called a general election, and to the surprise of both parties, the result was not just a Conservative victory but a landslide. For the first time since the fall of Peel, the Tories enjoyed a real majority in Parliament—and it was Peel's destroyer who would reap the benefits. It had taken nearly fifty years, but Disraeli finally achieved what Vivian Grey longed for: "Power! Oh! what sleepless nights, what days of hot anxiety! what exertions of mind and body! what travel! what hatred! what fierce encounters! what dangers of all possible kinds, would I not endure with a joyous spirit to gain it!"

Yet it is hard to escape the sense that Disraeli had endured too much, and waited too long, to make the most of power when he finally had it. When he began his second term as Prime Minister, Disraeli was sixty-nine years old, a widower, and in steadily worsening health. He would suffer throughout his term from bronchitis and gout, the disease that laid Derby low. ("All prime ministers have the gout," quipped a character in his last novel.) He could still revel in his victory—"The sense of power is delightful," he frankly acknowledged—but as he confided to Lady Bradford, power did not banish depression. "Perhaps, and probably, I ought to be pleased," he wrote. "I can only tell you the truth, which I always do, tho' to no one else. I am wearied to extinction and profoundly unhappy."

Age and low spirits were not Disraeli's only handicaps. He arrived at the summit of power with strikingly little executive experience. Though he had been in Parliament since 1837, he spent only four of those years in office. Now that his big chance had finally arrived, his Cabinet colleagues were surprised at how unprepared Disraeli seemed to be. R. A. Cross, his Home Secretary, remembered: "When the Cabinet came to discuss the Queen's Speech [in which the government announced its plans for the session], I was, I confess, disappointed at the want of originality shown by the Prime Minister. From all his speeches, I had quite expected that his mind was full of legislative schemes, but such did not prove to be the case; on the contrary, he had to entirely rely on the suggestions of his colleagues, and as they themselves had only just come into office, and that suddenly, there was some difficulty in framing the Queen's Speech."

Disraeli would remain a hands-off leader where legislation was concerned. "He detests details, he does no work," another cabinet member complained. But as it turned out, Disraeli's ability to delegate authority was one of his strengths as prime minister. He had already laid out his vision of a Conservative social-welfare policy; now he encouraged his cabinet to implement that vision in a number of important new laws. Among them were the Artisans' Dwellings Act, empowering local governments to clear slums and build public housing; the Employers and Workmen Act, making it legal for trade unions to strike; the Rivers Pollution Act, regulating the disposal of waste; the Sale of Food and Drugs Act, establishing standards of safety and purity; and the Factory Act, limiting the working hours of women and children. There were also new measures to safeguard the rights of agricultural tenants and sailors on merchant ships, to set aside a tract in London as a forest preserve, and to expand the system of free elementary education.

Late in Disraeli's term, Alexander Macdonald, one of the first Labour MPs, judged that "the Conservative party have done more for the working classes in five years than the Liberals have in fifty." It is an important reminder that the terms "conservative" and "liberal" meant something very different in Disraeli's time than they do in ours. Today, the small-government, pro-business principles of Victorian liberalism have their home in the American right wing, while our own liberals would find much to admire in the labor and environmental policies of Disraeli's Conservatives. At the same time, the principles Disraeli cherished most—class deference, the authority of tradition, imperialism—have virtually no salience in twenty-first-century American politics.

Though it was Disraeli's leadership that made all this social reform possible, he had little to do with drafting actual bills, preferring to concentrate on his real passion, which was foreign policy. As early as *Contarini Fleming*, he had dreamed of playing a role on the international stage: "Foreign policy opened a dazzling vista of splendid incident. It was enchanting to be acquainted with the secrets of European cabinets, and to control or influence their fortunes." One of the statesmen he most admired was Metternich, the archconservative Austrian chancellor who dominated the Congress of Vienna in 1815. Fate was to give Disraeli the chance to play the same role in an international conference of his own, the Congress of Berlin, where he helped to shape the future of Europe. But the crises leading up to the Congress, and the way he handled them, would also expose him to the most bitter criticism of his entire career. Once again, the sight of Disraeli exercising power led many Englishmen to doubt that he could be trusted with it.

There was at least one person, however, who could not have been more delighted to see Disraeli as prime minister, and hers was an opinion that counted. Queen Victoria and Disraeli had entered public life in the same year: her accession in 1837 prompted the election in which he got into Parliament. Her initial curiosity about this exotic figure turned to disgust after the fall of Peel, when she wrote that the House of Commons "ought to be ashamed of having such members as Lord George Bentinck and that detestable Mr. D'Israeli." This low opinion was reinforced by her beloved husband, Prince Albert. During the first Derby administration, the prince warned Derby that his lieutenant had the potential to be "one of the most dangerous men in Europe."

Albert was worried that Disraeli would become a radical democrat, an enemy of the established order. But this was a serious misjudgment, based more on suspicion of his origins than knowledge of his beliefs and political instincts. In fact, there was no more zealous defender of the monarchy than Disraeli. His devotion to the Crown had two powerful sources: his political philosophy, which led him to glorify the monarchy as the tribune of the people; and his poetic imagination, which allowed him to see the prosaic Victoria as a queen out of chivalric romance. This potent combination was already on display in *Sybil*, where he imagined the young Queen receiving her courtiers for the first time: "In a sweet and thrilling voice, and with a composed mien which indicates rather the absorbing sense of august duty than an absence of emotion, THE QUEEN announces her accession to the throne of her ancestors, and her humble hope that divine Providence will guard over the fulfilment of her lofty trust. . . . Will it be her proud destiny at length to bear relief to suffering millions, and, with that soft hand, which might inspire troubadours and guerdon knights, break the last links in the chain of Saxon thraldom?"

By the time Victoria was crowned, the days of troubadours and knights-at-arms were some five hundred years in the past. But Disraeli's hyperbole, while anachronistic, was not insincere. To politicians like Russell and Derby, who spent their whole lives in the same social sphere as royalty, and whose pedigrees were themselves only less than royal, the queen could be taken for granted as a rather average woman playing a necessary political role. To Disraeli, who saw her from a great social distance, she retained the poetry of a symbol—as she did for most of her subjects. And when he was able, against all odds, to close the distance between them, he never lost a sense of awe that a middle-class Jew should be the associate of an English monarch.

As a result, Disraeli treated the Queen with a genuine reverence, and a romantic fulsomeness, that none of her other prime ministers would have found appropriate. He had the further advantage of a novelist's gift for language, and he spiced his official correspondence with his characteristic poetry and wit. Each time he served as Leader of the House, it was one of his duties to write reports to the Queen on Parliamentary proceedings. She could not fail to notice the difference between the usual dry, bureaucratic account and Disraeli's racy narratives. One of the Queen's ladies-in-waiting remarked how Disraeli "writes daily letters to the Queen in his best novel style, telling her every scrap of political news dressed up to serve his own purpose, and every scrap of social gossip cooked to amuse her. She declares that she has never had such letters in her life, which is probably true, and that she never before knew *everything!*"

But it was the death of Prince Albert, in 1861, that really allowed Disraeli to win Victoria's confidence. Losing her husband was a life-changing trauma for the Queen. She relied on him in politics as in every other sphere, and in his absence she retreated from all her public responsibilities. In time she became so reclusive that the monarchy itself seemed to be in danger. But Disraeli, at this sensitive moment, knew exactly what the Queen wanted to hear, and since his admiration of Albert was genuine, he was not shy about praising the Prince's memory. In public, he thanked Albert for giving England "his thought, his time, his toil; he gave to it his life." In private he went even further, and an 1863 letter to the queen gives a good idea of the style he used with her:

> If, in venturing to touch upon a sacred theme, Mr. Disraeli may have, occasionally, used expressions which your Majesty has been graciously pleased to deem not altogther inadequate to the subject, he has been enabled to do so only because, on that subject, he speaks from the heart, and from long and frequent musing over its ever-living interest. . . . The Prince is the only person, whom Mr. Disraeli has ever known, who realized the Ideal. None with whom he is acquainted have ever approached it.

This is the kind of thing Disraeli must have had in mind when he told Matthew Arnold, "Everyone likes flattery; and, when you come to royalty, you should lay it on with a trowel." But Disraeli's treatment of the Queen was not as cynical as this suggests. He positively enjoyed flattering her, and still more, he enjoyed the spectacle of himself bending the knee to a Queen. If his flattery was not entirely sincere, it was insincere in the way of an idealized portrait: it perfectly expressed the way Disraeli thought a queen should be addressed by her loyal servant. Eventually he even began to refer to Victoria as "the Faery Queene," after Spenser's poem. In 1875, he thanked her for a gift of flowers by writing, "perhaps it was a Faery gift and came from another monarch: Queen Titania, gathering flowers, with her Court, in a soft and sea-girt isle, and sending magic blossoms, which, they say, turn the heads of those who receive them."

All this had the desired effect. During the 1860s, the man she once detested became Victoria's favorite politician. She sent Disraeli a book of Albert's speeches, with a letter expressing "her deep gratification at the tribute he paid to her adored, beloved, and great husband." She paid him the signal compliment of inviting him and Mary Anne to the exclusive wedding of the Prince of Wales, making Disraeli the envy of aristocratic society.

Their bond was sealed, however, in 1868, when Disraeli was named Prime Minister. For the rest of his term, and again when he was reelected, Disraeli wrote to and met with the Queen regularly. But he never grew inured to the experience, and he always addressed her with genuine excitement and respect. Increasingly, too, his chivalric devotion took on an amorous tone. Traditionally, when a new Prime Minister went to receive his appointment from the monarch, he was said to "kiss hands." But in 1876, after an important legislative victory, Disraeli kissed hands with the Queen quite literally. Saying "I think I may claim, Madam, the privilege of gratitude," Disraeli kissed her hand three times, and he recalled, "she actually gave me a squeeze." It is an odd but touching reminiscence of Disraeli's note to Mary Anne during their courtship, urging her to leave her hand bare so he could squeeze it. And when Victoria wrote about Disraeli's first visit to her after his reelection in 1874, she recorded his words almost breathlessly: "He repeatedly said *whatever I wished* SHOULD *be done.*"

There was no question, of course, of an actual romance between the Queen and her Prime Minister. Rather, Disraeli was using with Victoria the same techniques he had always used to win over older women. As with Sara Austen, Mary Anne, and Mrs. Brydges Willyams, he was inviting the Queen to receive his devotion and grant him approval. And the Queen, who was totally unapproachable in any ordinary romantic sense, responded to Disraeli's indirect flirtation. She granted him extraordinary privileges, even inviting him to remain seated in her presence—a favor that other Prime Ministers never received.

Naturally, not everyone was pleased by this intimacy. It was bad enough that the Queen, who was supposed to remain above party politics, so obviously preferred Disraeli to Gladstone, whom she found self-righteous and humorless. It was even worse that Disraeli had once again trespassed into a precinct where Jews were not supposed to enter. One Whig nobleman lamented that "the Jew, the most subtle beast in the field, has, like Eve's tempter, ingratiated himself with the Missus!" Eventually, Disraeli's relationship with the Queen even became a political issue. In 1876, he introduced the Royal Titles Bill, to officially add Empress of India to Victoria's title. The change had been considered for many years as a way to boost England's prestige in India, and specifically to give England's monarch the same imperial status as the Russian tsar. But many critics felt that the Bill was a product of Victoria's vanity, abetted by Disraeli's sycophancy; and it only passed after a difficult fight.

The Royal Titles Bill was a good example of the way a measure that might have looked innocuous, coming from any other politician, was suspect when it came from Disraeli. In his novels, he had often dwelled on his love of the East, his pride in his Eastern race, and "the great Asian mystery." All these things made it possible for his enemies to see in the Queen's new title evidence of a Disraelian plot to transform the British Empire into an Oriental despotism. Readers of *Tancred*, in particular, might have remembered a scene in which Fakredeen wildly advises: "Let the Queen of the English collect a great fleet, let her stow away all her treasure, bullion, gold plate, and precious arms; be accompanied by all her court and chief people, and transfer the seat of her empire from London to Delhi." The speech is intended as pure comedy, an example of Fakredeen's uncontrollable scheming. But now that Disraeli actually had the Queen's ear, it took on a sinister appearance.

It was not a long-laid plot, however, but an irony of history that the East actually did end up engrossing Disraeli's attention during his second term. At most, Disraeli's imaginative preoccupation with the East only left him better equipped to act boldly when the occasion demanded it. That was the case in 1875, when the bankrupt Khedive of Egypt

"NEW CROWNS FOR OLD ONES!"

(*Aladdin adapted.*)

Disraeli as Aladdin in a *Punch* cartoon on
the Royal Titles Bill.
*Courtesy of the Print Collection, Miriam and
Ira D. Wallach Division of Art, Prints,
and Photographs, The New York Public Library,
Astor, Lenox and Tilden Foundations.*

let it be known that he was ready to sell his shares in the
Suez Canal Company. A slight majority of the shares were
already owned by a French firm, and now another French
bidder proposed to buy the Khedive's holdings. The canal
had only been open for six years, but it was already a crucial
link between Britain and India, and Disraeli believed that
securing a British interest in the company was vital.

Disraeli's cabinet colleagues didn't want to pursue the matter, however, and in any case Parliament, which would need to vote the funds for the purchase, was out of session. The French bidder had an option that was about to expire, and if the British government couldn't come up with the money immediately, the Khedive would have to sell to the French. Now Disraeli's sense of drama, and his love of geopolitical intrigue, led him to take a bold step. In mid-November, he contacted the Rothschilds and asked for an immediate loan of £4 million to make the purchase. Montagu Corry, the prime minister's trusted secretary, left a dramatic, if not necessarily accurate, record of his interview with Lionel de Rothschild: when Rothschild asked "What is your security?" Corry replied, "The British Government." However it actually happened, the loan was made, and Britain bought the canal shares. Disraeli told the Queen the news in a typically theatrical letter: "It is just settled; you have it, Madam. The French Government has been out-generaled."

The Suez Canal intrigue is possibly the most celebrated episode in Disraeli's whole career. Yet the closer one looks at the facts, the less dramatic the whole thing appears. Disraeli did not, in fact, purchase "it," the canal, as he told the Queen. What he purchased was a minority share in the Company that collected the tolls from the canal; the majority of the company's shares remained in French hands. But in any case, the company never had the power to close the canal or prevent any nation's ships from using it. If France, Egypt, or anyone else tried to close the Suez Canal, Britain would have to go to war to keep it open, whether it owned the shares or not. Nor did Disraeli put one over on France. In fact, the French government had already agreed not to support a French bid for the shares, in deference to Britain's wishes.

In short, Disraeli's coup was mostly symbolic. But it was his own imaginative persona that made the symbolism effective. Any British government would have considered the Suez Canal a vital interest; but because Disraeli had long positioned himself as an "Eastern" figure, his concern for the canal looked like part of a grand design to increase Britain's power in the East. His decisive action to secure the shares became the dramatic escapade of a born novelist.

Above all, his resort to the Rothschilds played into the fantasy of Jewish power Disraeli had elaborated in his novels. The Rothschilds' loan was actually a straightforward and lucrative business decision—as soon as Parliament reconvened, the loan was repaid, with a tidy profit (a little too tidy, in the eyes of some critics). But because Disraeli had invented Sidonia, the whole transaction took on a Sidonian air—the ultimate example of secret Jewish connections at work behind the scenes. Disraeli's actions as prime minister had little to do with his fantasies and fictions, but the public interpretation of those actions did. The price of creating his own myth was that he had to live inside it.

16

On August 11, 1876, Disraeli made his last speech in the House of Commons. The next day, it was announced that the Queen had created him Earl of Beaconsfield. It was age and sickness, not vanity, that led Disraeli to accept a title. During the previous session, parliamentary business had dragged because of the Prime Minister's feebleness. As a peer, he could lead the government from the House of Lords, where the pace of business was slower, and leave the hard work of debate and party management to his lieutenants. At first he had even floated the idea of resigning from office; but this was one of his favorite stratagems for keeping supporters in line, and he could not have been disappointed when the cabinet insisted that he remain in power. "There are some excellent heads and hearts in the Cabinet, but only one backbone," one Minister told him.

There was a delicate irony in the title that Disraeli chose for himself. Beaconsfield was the name of a village near Hughenden, and it may have appealed to him because of its associations with the great conservative Edmund Burke, who died there. But he surely also remembered, even if no one else did, that in *Vivian Grey* he had used the name Beaconsfield for a character who is mentioned in passing.

"There is Beaconsfield, but we are not intimate," says the Marquis of Carabas as he reviews his possible allies. By taking the name for himself, Disraeli seemed to be insisting once again on the imaginative continuity of his life. He had managed to translate his fantasy of becoming prime minister, that impossible goal of his early novels, into reality; the statesman known as Lord Beaconsfield was Disraeli's creation, as surely as any of the characters in his books.

Disraeli's departure from the Commons seemed to mark an epoch in Victorian politics. He had been a member of the House for almost forty years, and it was already clear that he would go down in history as one of the greatest parliamentarians who ever lived. The very fact that he spent most of his career in the Opposition meant that his reputation rested more on his skill as a debater than on his talents as a leader. His foreign appearance and inscrutable demeanor, which provoked so much suspicion over the years, had evolved into fixtures of parliamentary life. Certainly no MP in 1837 could have predicted that the MPs of 1876 would be so sorry to see Disraeli go. "All the real chivalry and delight of party politics seem to have departed," one wrote to him. "Nothing remains but routine."

If Disraeli hoped that his elevation to the Lords would begin a quieter period in his life, however, he was to be disappointed. The last speech he delivered in the Commons dealt with a controversy that was already beginning to inflame British opinion, and that would embitter politics for the next two years. This was the latest eruption of the so-called Eastern Question—which was, at bottom, the problem of how to manage the decline of the Ottoman Empire. The Turks, who during the Renaissance had advanced to the gates of Vienna, suffered a steady decline starting in the eighteenth century. Their military and political weakness opened up a power vacuum in southeastern Europe, provoking a series of wars and diplomatic crises throughout the nineteenth century.

The powers most immediately concerned with the fate of Turkey were its neighbors, Russia and Austria-Hungary. But Britain also considered the Eastern Question vital, primarily on account of India. In theory, if Russia expanded into Central Asia or seized Constantinople, she could cut the British route to India, imperiling the "jewel in the crown" of Empire. The extended duel between Britian and Russia over the future of the region was what Rudyard Kipling, in *Kim*, called "the Great Game."

Ever since Palmerston, it had been British policy to try to keep the Ottoman Empire intact as a bulwark against Russia. That had been the motivation behind the Crimean War, in which Britain and France joined Turkey to resist the Tsar. But in 1876, a series of events started to change the way many Britons thought about this traditional strategy. Over the previous year, the Balkans had been in turmoil, as the Slavic Christian subjects and neighbors of Turkey grew more and more determined to resist the crumbling Empire. In June, a London newspaper published an account of a horrifying massacre perpetrated by Muslim Turkish soldiers against Bulgarian Christians. Some twelve thousand civilians had been killed, including women and children, in a gruesome campaign of slaughter, pillage, and rape.

The news outraged the conscience of Britain, but it put Disraeli and his government in a sensitive position. During the diplomatic crises of the past year, Britain had emerged as Turkey's major ally. Disraeli refused to join the other great powers in plans for reforming the Sultan's government, which he feared would end by dismembering the Ottoman Empire. Now he saw that the Bulgarian atrocities, as they were called, might provoke so much anger against the Turks that his own people would no longer tolerate a pro-Turkish policy. And if Britain turned against Turkey, he feared, the whole system of British foreign policy might collapse, leading to a dangerous expansion of Russian power.

In short, Disraeli urgently wanted the atrocity stories not to be true. When the issue was raised in the House of Commons, he haughtily dismissed it, predicting that "when we are thoroughly informed of what has occurred, it will be found that [the stories] are scarcely warranted." Then he went on to use language he would regret. "I cannot doubt that atrocities have been committed in Bulgaria," he acknowledged, "but that girls were sold into slavery, or that more than 10,000 persons have been imprisoned, I doubt. In fact, I doubt whether there is prison accommodation for so many, or that torture has been practiced on a great scale among an Oriental people who seldom, I believe, resort to torture, but generally terminate their connection with culprits in a more expeditious manner."

Disraeli always claimed that this was not meant as a specimen of his typical sarcasm. When his speech provoked laughter in the House, he turned to a colleague and said angrily, "What is there to laugh at?" But the damage was done: Disraeli had created the impression that he was mocking the Christian victims of persecution. For any Prime Minister, this would have been a public relations blunder; for Disraeli, it was a disaster. Over the next few months, as further reports left no doubt that the Bulgarian atrocities were genuine, British public opinion rose to a high pitch of moral outrage. And along with the Turks, their own "Eastern" prime minister would become a central target. As the *Times* editorialized, "the more worthy part of English society was deeply pained by the frivolity of the Prime Minister's speech, as well as by the evident desire to diminish or excuse what had happened."

The Bulgarian controversy was perfectly calculated to damage Disraeli, since it touched on his greatest political vulnerability. The British public, which was more than content to see its government employ violence against the subject races of the British Empire, was moved to fury by the spectacle of Muslim Turks killing Christian Slavs. The religious element transformed the massacres from a humanitarian crime into a clash of civilizations, and allowed the Protestant British to identify themselves closely with the Orthodox Bulgarians. The "atrocitarians," as they were called, hammered on this point again and again, resorting to the medieval language of "Christendom" to rally the people against "the Turk." One politician spoke of the need to "emancipate Europe from the curse which afflicted her, and redeem Christendom from the shame by which she had been too long dishonored." At St. Paul's Cathedral, a preacher announced that "silence is impossible without a manifest disloyalty to the cause of Christ."

And there was no doubt about who was guilty of disloyalty to the cause of Christ. Didn't it make perfect sense that the Jewish prime minister would now fail to heed the cry of suffering Christians? Disraeli's anti-atrocitarian stand was shared by many politicians, and no one endorsed it more heartily than Queen Victoria, who could not fathom "this mawkish sentimentality for people who hardly deserve the name of real Christians." But to Disraeli's enemies, it was obvious that Jewishness, not politics or diplomacy, was the real explanation for his views. England had allowed itself to be led by an alien, and now that alien was perverting the people's moral instincts. Such was the barely veiled message of the St. Paul's preacher, Canon Liddon:

It may fairly be pleaded for the Power which has perpetrated these acts that it knows not the name of Christ, and that its proceedings are not to be judged by the standard of a European and Christian civilization. Be it so; but that which makes the voice falter as we say it is that, through whatever misunderstanding, the Government which is immediately responsible for acts like these has turned for sympathy, for encouragement, not to any of the historical houses of despotism or oppression, not to any other European Power, but alas to England—to free, humane Christian England. The Turk has, not altogether without reason, believed himself, amid these scenes of cruelty, to be sure of her smile, or at least of her acquiescence.

One major strand of the atrocitarians' rhetoric, then, was the need for England to impress her Christian principles on her erring leader. *Punch* ran a cartoon showing the British Lion upbraiding Disraeli: "Look here, I don't understand *you*! But it's right you should understand *me*! *I don't fight to uphold what's going on yonder!*" The great Liberal John Bright attacked "the betrayal of a Minister who has not one single drop of English blood in his veins." E. A. Freeman, one of Disraeli's most extreme foes, went still further. "Whether we are a majority, I cannot tell: but I am sure we are a large enough part of the English people to make even the Jew in his drunken insolence think twice," he wrote. Later, when the queen paid a visit to Hughenden, Freeman denounced her for "going ostentatiously to eat with Disraeli in his ghetto."

But the critic whose self-righteousness infuriated Disraeli most was his old rival Gladstone. After the election of 1874, Gladstone had given up the leadership of the Liberal Party. But he remained the most important Liberal in the country, and those who knew him doubted that he could remain out of politics for long. Now Gladstone, a deeply pious Christian, was driven by the Bulgarian atrocities to reenter the

"NO MISTAKE!"

The British Lion upbraids the Sphinx Disraeli over the
Bulgarian atrocities.

*Courtesy of the Print Collection, Miriam and Ira D. Wallach Division of Art,
Prints, and Photographs, The New York Public Library, Astor, Lenox and
Tilden Foundations.*

public arena. He did so in spectacular fashion, with his pamphlet *The Bulgarian Horrors and the Question of the East*. Written in three days, the tract went on to sell more than two hundred thousand copies, making Gladstone effectively the spokesman for the Turcophobe party. After painting the atrocities in lurid colors, Gladstone framed the geopolitical issue as a Manichaean contest between the forces of Christian humanity and the incorrigible evil of the Muslim Turks. The Turks "were, upon the whole, from the black day when they first entered Europe, the one great anti-human specimen of humanity," he wrote. He concluded with a call for what amounted to ethnic cleansing: "Let the Turks now carry away their abuses in the only possible manner, namely by carrying off themselves . . . one and all, bag and baggage."

Gladstone's pamphlet offers a perfect example of the way an admirable moral passion can be morally blinding. He revels in his own righteousness to the extent of denying his enemies' very humanity. Nor does he reckon in any way with the practical consequences of "carrying off" the Turks, or what would happen to the Balkans if Turkish domination were replaced by Russian and Austrian domination. What most irritated Disraeli, however, was the way Gladstone set himself up as the government's moral tutor. "The British Government have misunderstood, and therefore have misrepresented, the sense of the British people," he wrote. "The nation . . . must first teach its Government, almost as it would teach a lisping child, what to say."

Gladstone did not descend to the open anti-Semitism of some of Disraeli's critics. But in private, he left no doubt that he believed Disraeli's Jewishness was responsible for his "misrepresentation" of the popular feeling. "What [he] hates is Christian liberty," Gladstone wrote to one political ally. "Dizzy is of course looking for the weak side of the English people, on which he has thriven so long," he complained to another, adding, "we are governed on Asiatic principles." When the question of an early dissolution of Parliament arose, Gladstone spoke about Disraeli in still less flattering terms: "B[eaconsfield] if he is to disappear, would rather disappear in flame and stench," like the devil.

There was, however, a potentially more sympathetic way of connecting Disraeli's Jewishness with his foreign policy. Gladstone suggested it when he wrote, "I have a strong suspicion that Dizzy's crypto-Judaism has had to do with his policy. The Jews of the East *bitterly* hate the Christians; who have not always used them well." On this view, Disraeli opposed the Russians not because of British national interests but out of resentment against the tsar's persecution of his Jewish subjects. In fact, English Jews, who were traditionally Liberals, largely opposed the Liberal Russophile position for exactly this reason. When they saw how abysmally the Jews were treated in Romania, a Slavic state carved out of the Ottoman Empire, they were not eager to see more such nations on the map.

But to analyze Disraeli's policy in these terms is fundamentally to mistake the way he thought about his responsibilities as a Jew and a statesman. In his novels, Disraeli had imagined himself in the role of a Jewish national leader. But the proto-Zionist possibilities of *Alroy* and *Tancred* represented, for Disraeli, the road not taken. Once he embarked on his career as an English politician, he took great care not to be associated with Jewish causes. How sensitive he was on this subject can be gauged by his response when it was suggested to him that he recommend Moses Montefiore for a peerage. He was "less than any other Prime Minister in a position to grant the request," Disraeli replied. For all his hints about subterranean Jewish power, even the slightest appearance of using the actual power of the British state to promote Jewish interests made him shrink in horror.

(Indeed, it would be Gladstone who named the first Jewish peer.)

In fact, the logic of Disraeli's stance on the Bulgarian atrocities made it impossible for him to use his political position to advance collective Jewish aims. The main reason he dismissed the Bulgarian grievances was that he instinctively favored established, multinational empires over national liberation movements. Whether it was Greece rising against Turkey, Italy against Austria, or Poland against Russia, Disraeli always sided with the powers that were. And it seems clear that this preference was intimately bound up with his understanding of his own Jewishness.

After all, if the nation were a valid political unit, then working for its liberation would be a political imperative, and Disraeli's destiny would have to lie with the Jewish nation. He would have to follow the Zionist path that tempted him as early as *Alroy*. But by the time he created the character of Sidonia, Disraeli had decided that he could not and would not pursue that path. Instead, he would devote himself to the British Empire, even while recognizing that he could never belong to the English nation in the most intimate sense. He evolved his theory of race partly to justify this course to himself. For if the Jews were a race, not a nation, then they had a biological solidarity that religious and political "apostasy" could not violate. Individual Jews could exercise their talents in the service of imperial governments while still doing credit to their race—just as Sidonia's gifts, while employed in the Diaspora, served as an advertisment for Jewish power.

By the time of the Bulgarian atrocities, Disraeli's allegiances had been settled for several decades. He would not be governed in such a crucial moment by Jewish loyalties, only by British interests. Inevitably, when his critics suggested that he misunderstood those interests, by conceiving of them in terms of power rather than justice, Disraeli bridled. The more passionate his critics became, in fact, the more defiantly he stuck to his original position, and the more flippantly he spoke about the atrocities. In Parliament, he dismissed "that coffee-house babble brought by an anonymous Bulgarian." He joked that Gladstone's pamphlet was "of all the Bulgarian horrors, perhaps the greatest." He even wrote Lady Bradford from Hughenden, "I am almost thinking of perpetrating a sort of atrocity here, and massacring the peacocks."

This kind of callousness was not just in poor taste. It also hints at the high cost of Disraeli's habit of identifying himself with the powerful instead of the powerless. When his opponents brought up the genuine and terrible suffering of the Bulgarians, he could not allow himself to feel it. Even on the assumption that his pro-Turkish policy was the right one, a public show of sympathy with the Bulgarian Christians would have made his political course much easier. Instead, Disraeli immediately changed the terms of the discussion from morality to geopolitics, acting as though the Bulgarians were too insignificant to be weighed in the scale of empires. Doing otherwise might have compelled him to ask whether the scale of empires is a true one, and what purpose empires serve if they batten on the suffering of actual human beings. In short, he might have been brought to wonder whether greatness, the aesthetic category that had always fueled his ambitions, was really preferable to justice. At this late date in Disraeli's career, it would have been too severe a self-interrogation.

The moral passions aroused by the Bulgarian atrocities did not die down. For the next two years, British politics would be divided into Turcophile and Russophile factions, loosely identified with the Conservative and Liberal parties, respectively. According to one observer, politics was more acrimonious than at any time in living memory: "Friends of years standing become bitter foes—members of the same family don't speak one to the other—and when the questions are discussed, which they are morning noon and night by all classes and by both sexes there is an intensity of excitement that frequently breaks out into the most violent language—and it is all *purely personal*, the divergence of opinion not being so much upon the merits of the question which seem seldom understood, but upon the feelings that are entertained either towards Lord Beaconsfield or Mr. Gladstone."

The question at the heart of the debate was how Britain should respond to the escalating crisis in the Balkans. In April 1877, Russia declared war on Turkey, claiming to be acting as the protector of the sultan's Orthodox subjects. Britain responded by announcing that a Russian attack on

Constantinople would be considered a violation of her own vital interests. Public opinion began to swing around to Disraeli's hard-line policy, and a popular music hall song coined a word that was to have a great future: "We don't want to fight, but, by Jingo, if we do,/We've got the ships, we've got the men, we've got the money too."

The problem was that British opinion had turned so strongly against the Turks that it seemed impossible for Disraeli to actually bring the country into a war on the Turkish side. To fight alongside the Muslim perpetrators of atrocities, against the Christian power that was protecting their victims, appeared to many Englishmen like an abomination. Gladstone explicitly declared, "My purpose has been . . . to the best of my power, for the last eighteen months, day and night, week by week, month by month, to counterwork as well as I could what I believe to be the purpose of Lord Beaconsfield." It was not just the Liberals who found Disraeli's bellicose policy alarming. When he insisted on asking Parliament for a large credit to begin mobilizing troops, and ordered the British fleet to the Dardanelles, his own foreign secretary—the new Earl of Derby, the former Stanley, son of Disraeli's old chief—resigned in disagreement.

By early 1878, the Russians had defeated the Turks, and it was too late for Disraeli to prevent the Ottoman Empire from being sliced up. But the Russian Army had not yet moved on Constantinople, and Disraeli meant to make sure his ultimatum was respected. He moved ahead with military preparations, and in April took the unusual—and to his critics, unconstitutional—step of ordering troops from India to the Mediterranean. He was consciously risking a repetition of the Crimean War, which Britain would have to fight this time without France at her side. In his own eyes, this was a risk worth taking, for the sake of defending Britain's route to India and maintaining her credibility as a great power.

Yet even this stance, which if anything represented an excessive zeal for British interests, was inevitably attributed by some to Disraeli's "foreignness." Derby had once been Disraeli's political protégé; they had known each other and worked together for thirty years. But now even he turned against his mentor with the old accusation that Disraeli could never truly understand England, because he could never be English. "He believes thoroughly in 'prestige' as all foreigners do," Derby wrote, "and would think it (quite sincerely) in the interests of the country to spend 200 millions on a war if the result was to make foreign States think more highly of us as a military power." The same policy that had made Palmerston a hero looked "foreign" when pursued by a Jewish prime minister.

Still, Disraeli followed his aggressive course with his eyes open. The queen supported him ardently, and their correspondence during these tense months reached a new pitch of intimacy. "He feels there is no devotion that your Majesty does not deserve," Disraeli wrote in February 1878, "and he only wishes he had youth and energy to be the fitting champion of such an inspiring Mistress as your Majesty." Both of them agreed that Britain could only negotiate with Russia from a position of strength. "When all Europe was armed," Disraeli asked in the House of Lords, "was England to be disarmed?"

In the end, Disraeli's brinkmanship proved successful: Russia did not cross the Dardanelles, and war was averted. There still remained, however, the problem of drawing a new map of the Balkans, now that much Turkish territory had been lost. The Treaty of San Stefano, which the Russians dictated to the Turks, was highly punitive, in ways that especially alarmed Britain. It gave Russia a large swath of territory in Asia Minor, and in the Balkans it created a huge new state of Bulgaria, which threatened to become a Russian proxy.

It was in the aftermath of the Treaty that Disraeli scored his greatest diplomatic success. His determined policy, combined with pressure from the other great powers, compelled Russia to allow a diplomatic conference to settle the postwar borders. The Congress of Berlin opened in June 1878, bringing together all the leading statesmen in Europe. Disraeli was extremely frail—"the Kingdom was never governed with such an amount of catarrh and sneezing," he wrote to Lady Bradford—but he resolved to attend in person. Salisbury, once Disraeli's fierce critic, now his new Foreign Secretary, did most of the actual work. "What with deafness, ignorance of French and Bismarck's extraordinary mode of speech," he grumbled, "Beaconsfield has the dimmest idea of what is going on."

But it was Disraeli who was the star of the Congress. No

statesman deserved more credit for stopping Russia's advance and bringing her to the negotiating table. Even one Liberal politician admitted, "England now holds as proud a position as she ever had; and that is due to the sagacity, and power, and conduct of the despised person once called Benjamin Disraeli." Disraeli's exotic origins and romantic career made him a celebrity at Berlin. "What amuses me rather," he bragged, "is that almost everybody, certainly all the ladies, are reading my novels, from the Empress downwards. The ladies are generally reading *Henrietta Temple*, which being a 'love story' and written forty years ago, is hardly becoming an Envoy Extraordinary." Bismarck, a statesman Disraeli admired, summed up the general opinion: "*Der alte Jude, das ist der Mann*," "The old Jew, that is a man."

Disraeli achieved enough of his diplomatic objectives to consider the Congress a great success. The "big Bulgaria" designed by Russia was broken in two, and its borders adjusted to the advantage of Turkey. An even more spectacular coup, however, was Britain's acquisition of the island of Cyprus, which Turkey handed over for use as a base to resist future Russian aggression. This was denounced as a land-grab by Disraeli's critics, including Gladstone, who called it "insane." But it was exactly the kind of bold stroke that delighted Disraeli. Ever since he was a teenager, he had dreamed about wielding power over the fates of nations. Now he was singlehandedly expanding the borders of the British Empire.

In July, after the final treaty was signed in Berlin, Disraeli returned home to a hero's welcome. Cheering crowds escorted him from the train station back to Downing Street, and he appeared at the window to thank them: "Lord Salisbury and myself have brought you back peace, but a peace, I hope, with honour, which may satisfy our Sovereign and tend to the welfare of the country." It was to this speech that Neville Chamberlain referred when, on his return from Munich in 1938, he made Disraeli's phrase infamous: "My good friends, for the second time in our history, a British Prime Minister has returned from Germany bringing peace with honour. I believe it is peace for our time."

In fact, Chamberlain's ignominious surrender to the Nazis offered a perfect contrast to Disraeli's achievement, for Disraeli's honorable peace was owed to his readiness to go to war in defense of what he considered a crucial principle. He demonstrated the importance of what he called "that force which it is necessary to possess often in great transactions, though fortunately you may not feel that it is necessary to have recourse to that force." In the 1930s, it was clearly Winston Churchill, the advocate of rearmament and the foe of appeasement, who spoke for Disraelian values.

In a broader sense, too, Churchill's vision of the greatness and goodness of the British Empire, which sustained him during the worst moments of the Second World War, owes much to Disraeli's romantic imperialism. While their origins could not have been more different—Churchill was a descendant of one of the greatest men in English history, the Duke of Marlborough—the two prime ministers had in common something more important than pedigree. They were both writers—indeed, they were the only major writers to hold the office—and they understood their country poetically as well as politically. Of Churchill, too, it could be said that England was the Israel of his imagination.

In some of his wartime speeches, Churchill even seemed consciously to invoke Disraeli's powerful vision of British destiny. Speaking in the House of Commons on September 3, 1939, the day war was declared against Germany, Churchill countered Chamberlain's expression of regret with "a feeling of thankfulness that, if these great trials were to come upon our Island, there is a generation of Britons here now ready to prove itself not unworthy of the days of yore and not unworthy of those great men, the fathers of our land, who laid the foundations of our laws and shaped the greatness of our country." It was an unmistakable echo of the famous speech Disraeli delivered in November 1878, celebrating his Berlin triumph and rebuking those "who think that the power of England is on the wane. . . . I feel confident, if England is true to herself, if the English people prove themselves worthy of their ancestors, if they possess still the courage and determination of their forefathers, their honour will never be tarnished and their power will never diminish."

In the most dangerous passage of modern British history, Churchill turned to Disraeli, consciously or not, for the language of pride and endurance. That Disraeli's "forefathers" were not those of his audience, that he was lauding ancestral virtues many Englishmen believed he could not share, only makes Churchill's use of his imagery the more moving. Indeed, Churchill himself gave tribute, on one remarkable occasion, to the power Disraeli exercised over his imagination. In November 1947, he recorded, he had a dream that he was talking with his father, Randolph Churchill, who emerged as a leading Conservative politician during the last years of Disraeli's life. "I always believed in Dizzy, that old Jew," Randolph told his son in the dream. "He saw into the future."

In the long term, it is not clear whether the Congress of Berlin was really the triumph for England that it appeared at the time. Historians continue to question whether Disraeli's tough stance actually deterred Russia from crossing the Dardanelles, or whether, as it later appeared from the diplomatic archives, the tsar's war aims had been limited from the beginning. Certainly the acquisition of Cyprus proved to be an albatross. It never served the British as an important base, while in the 1950s, it involved them in a bloody counterinsurgency against the Cypriot independence movement. More broadly, it is unclear whether the survival of the Ottoman Empire was really a vital British interest, as Disraeli firmly believed. Even at the time, some analysts thought that the old fear of the Russians cutting the British link to India was a phantom.

Perhaps if Britain had joined the other European powers

in dismantling Turkey, instead of trying to prop it up, the subsequent history of Europe would have been different. For the Congress of Berlin did not manage to bring a lasting settlement to the Balkans. Bosnia would provide the flash point for the First World War in 1914. Even in our own day, the ethnic warfare in the former Yugoslavia is a legacy of Europe's failure to find a real solution to the Eastern Question. Still, when he returned home from Berlin in 1878, Disraeli's exaltation was justified. He had carried through a risky policy to a successful conclusion, despite determined opposition; he had protected what he believed to be Britain's interests; he had helped to preserve the European balance of power for a generation. And he had done it all through the sheer power of his will—the same will that had enabled him to rise from obscurity to world fame. A lifetime earlier, in *Contarini Fleming*, he confessed his "deep conviction that life must be intolerable unless I were the greatest of men." Now, for a moment at least, he was.

17

In his last speech in the House of Commons, Disraeli declared, "What our duty is at this critical moment is to maintain the Empire of England." At the Congress of Berlin, it appeared that he had delivered on his promise. He reiterated his imperialist views in an 1879 speech, when he coined another slogan: "One of the greatest of Romans, when asked what were his politics, replied, *Imperium et Libertas.* That would not make a bad programme for a British Ministry." But as the last two years of his government were to show, Empire and Liberty were ultimately irreconcilable values.

After narrowly avoiding a war with Russia, the last thing Disraeli wanted was further intrigues in the Great Game. But in the same month as the Congress of Berlin, tensions erupted in Afghanistan, the country that lay between Russia and British India. The Amir of Afghanistan infuriated the British by receiving an official mission from the tsar in Kabul. London warned Lord Lytton, Disraeli's handpicked viceroy, not to respond aggressively, hoping to avoid committing British forces while they were already overextended. But Lytton defied orders, sending an armed mission of his own into Afghanistan. When it was turned back at the border, he responded with a full-scale invasion. The Second Afghan War, as it was called, succeeded in ousting the Amir and replacing him with his son.

The affair renewed tensions with Russia at the worst possible moment, and it exasperated Disraeli, who blamed Lytton for exceeding his authority. The truth was, however, that the imperial system necessarily delegated the authority to make war to local governors, at a time when communication with London could take days or weeks. And the logic of imperialism, of Disraeli's cherished "Empire of England," entailed ever-renewed conflict. As the Afghan War showed, the imperial borders could not remain static but would be continually pushed forward in order to defend previously conquered territory.

The same dynamic was at work in South Africa, where another border war broke out a few months later. Once again, the governor, Sir Bartle Frere, exceeded his orders by attacking a neighboring power, believing that aggression was the best defense. This time the enemy was the Zulus, who proved more formidable than the Afghans. In January 1879, a Zulu army annihilated a force of twelve hundred British troops at Isandlwana, creating a military crisis and a political disaster for Disraeli. He had never wanted the Zulu War in the first place, and he made his anger at Frere publicly known.

Disraeli's political imagination had always been his greatest strength. It was what allowed him to see the Tory Party as a national party when it seemed doomed to reactionary obsolescence and to see himself as a vindicator of English traditions when to all appearances he was an alien. But now, his vivid imagination of imperial glory proved to be almost too convincing. It gave the impression that the war in South Africa, the war in Afghanistan, and the brinkmanship over Constantinople were all part of a deliberate policy, rather than a series of emergencies that Disraeli struggled to contain.

Gladstone, for one, believed that Disraeli was pursuing a definite ideology, which he denounced as "Beaconsfieldism." In late 1879, Gladstone returned to active politics in his legendary Midlothian campaign, delivering a series of fiery speeches to huge audiences in Scotland. His chief subject, as it had been for the previous three years, was the iniquity of Disraeli, whom he accused of having led the English astray. A prime minister's duty, he lectured, was "not to set up false phantoms of glory which are to delude [the people] into calamity, not to flatter their infirmities by leading them to believe that they are better than the rest of the world . . . but to proceed upon a principle that recognizes the sisterhood and equality of nations." He urged his listeners to "recollect the sacred name we bear as Christians," and to "resolve . . . before God and before man" to reject the "mischievous and ruinous misdeeds" of Disraeli's government. He called down the vengeance of Britain on her seducer: "The nation is a power hard to rouse," he thundered, "but when roused, harder still and more hopeless to resist."

The attacks were so unremitting and drew on such power-ful religious tropes, that even Disraeli's armor of aloofness was pierced. He shot back at Gladstone, calling him "a sophistical rhetorician, inebriated with the exuberance of his own verbosity and gifted with an egotistical imagination that can at all times command an interminable and inconsis-tent series of arguments to malign an opponent and to glo-rify himself." In private, he referred to him as "A.V.," for Arch Villain. The fire was stoked by Queen Victoria, who had come to loathe Gladstone as intensely as Disraeli did. "She would sooner *abdicate* than send for or have anything to do with that *half-mad fire-brand*," the queen raged.

But events left her no choice. If Disraeli had called a gen-eral election in 1878, after his Berlin triumph, the Conserva-tives would probably have won easily. But he waited until the spring of 1880, and by then the tide had turned. Glad-stone's success in Midlothian crowned a Liberal victory, in which the Tories lost more than a hundred seats. The wars in Afghanistan and South Africa had something to do with the debacle, and so did Gladstone's moral crusade. But it was an economic slump, including several years of agricultural depression, that sealed the Conservatives' fate. "I think, as far as I can collect, 'hard times' was the cry against us. The suffering want a change—no matter what, they are sick of waiting," Disraeli explained.

In April 1880, after six years in power, Disraeli left office for the last time. He and the queen almost sounded like parted lovers. "His relations with your Majesty were his chief, he might almost say his only, happiness and interest in this world," he told her; and hyperbole aside, he was telling the truth. Victoria was the only woman left him to flatter and impress, and playing the role of her champion had been one of the most gratifying adventures of his life. Her own sorrow was equally sincere, as she proved by taking the extraordinary step of writing to him in the first person: "When we correspond—which I hope we shall on many a *private* subject and without anyone being astonished or offended . . . I hope it will be in this more easy form."

Disraeli continued as leader of the Conservative Party. But he was seventy-five years old and in poor health, and he must have recognized that he would not live to see another general election. Instead of devoting his remaining energies to politics, then, he turned one last time to his first calling, literature. He resumed work on a novel he had begun to sketch just after *Lothair*, and in September he delivered the manuscript of *Endymion*. His fee for the book was £10,000, an unheard-of figure that reflected the public fascination: never before or since has a statesman of Disraeli's stature published a serious work of fiction. Characteristically, he never worried that he might squander in novel writing the dignity he had earned in politics. He was too proud to abjure any part of his personality, and he recognized that his novelistic imagination had played a large role in his political success.

There was even, perhaps, a certain satisfaction in reminding the world that, while Gladstone had written many books on history and theology, he could never write a novel.

"There is not a form of literature which this man is not attempting," Disraeli once sneered, "except a work of fiction—the test of all talents. . . . Nothing can be more unmusical, more involved, or more uncouth than all his scribblement; he has not produced a page which you can put on your library shelves."

In his first novel, Disraeli had fantasized about the political career he believed was in store for him. Now, in his last, he wrote elegiacally about the career he was leaving behind. Like his creator, Endymion Ferrars is a young man making his way in politics in the 1830s and 1840s. This setting allows Disraeli to reminisce about the political world of his own early days and to satirize it gently. Zenobia, a grand hostess, expresses the arrogance of her falling class: when someone explains the concept of "public opinion" to her, she scoffs, "How very absurd! a mere nickname. As if there could be any opinion but that of the Sovereign and the two Houses of Parliament." This was the smug voice of the pre-Reform Tories, and Disraeli was one of the last men in politics who could remember it.

Through Endymion, Disraeli relives his own years of apprenticeship—the political gossip, the rivalrous friendships, even the fear of public speaking. "Endymion for the first time heard his own voice in public," Disraeli writes. "He has since admitted, though he has been through many trying scenes, that it was the most nervous moment of his life." Above all, Endymion shares the ambition that is the hallmark of all Disraeli's heroes. When an older man advises him, "You may have success in life without stepping out of the crowd," he replies: "But what I mean is real success in life. I mean, I should like to be a public man." Yet Endymion, who is a Whig during the period of Whig ascendancy, is able to gratify his ambition much more easily than Disraeli did. By the end of the novel, Endmyion is not yet middle-aged, and he has just been named prime minister.

This rise is made possible by his twin sister, Myra, who is by far the more compelling character. If Disraeli assigns Endymion his own ambition, he endows Myra with his unrelenting determination. She will do anything and sacrifice anything for her brother's sake. "I have brought myself, by long meditation, to the conviction that a human being with a settled purpose must accomplish it, and that nothing can resist a will that will stake even existence for its fulfillment," she declares. Myra advances Endymion's career by marrying Lord Roehampton, the elderly statesman who is Disraeli's version of Lord Palmerston; then, when he dies, she ascends even higher, marrying Prince Florestan, a stand-in for Napoléon III. This fantastic career seems like Disraeli's way of paying homage to the women who made his own rise possible—his sister, his wife, and even his Queen. Women, he reminds his readers, are able to exercise political power even when they are deprived of political rights. "Everything in this world depends upon will," another hostess tells Endymion, who demurs, "I think everything in this world depends upon woman." "It is the same thing," she replies.

Perhaps the most significant thing about Myra, however,

is the motivation behind her almost frightening resolve. Myra and Endymion's father was himself a Cabinet minister, and their early years were spent in privilege in London. But their father fell from power after the Reform Bill, went bankrupt, and ended up committing suicide. The easygoing Endymion was able to bear up under these shocks, but to the proud Myra, they were intolerable: "I feel as if we had fallen from some star," she says. Her one purpose in life is to retrieve her lost patrimony. "We must never forget the great object for which we two live," she tells Endymion, "for which, I believe, we were born twins—to rebuild our house; to raise it from poverty, and ignominy, and misery and squalid shame, to the rank and position which we demand, and which we believe we deserve."

It is a legible metaphor for Disraeli's own experience as a Jew. He, too, grew up knowing that he was mysteriously disgraced—that his birth had placed him near the bottom of English society, even though his gifts urged him toward the top. His great imaginative triumph, the one on which all his worldly triumphs rested, was to reimagine his Jewishness as a glorious inheritance. Yet while Myra's goal is to rebuild "our house," Disraeli was torn between the possibilities of collective and individual redemption. As early as *Alroy*, he had seen that the destiny of David Alroy—the redeemer of the Jewish people, the restorer of the Jewish state—was incompatible with that of Honain, who was his own messiah. In the end, his own powers, and the possibilities his world offered him, led Disraeli to take the second course. He followed it to the most glorious possible conclusion, but it remained a personal glory, and Disraeli is still remembered as a great exception in European history. More than a century and a quarter after his death, he is still the only Jew to be prime minister of England.

Disraeli's understanding of Jewishness was deeply distorted by his disconnection from the collective Jewish life of his time. Eventually, those distortions even played into the hands of the enemies of the Jews, when they took Sidonia, Disraeli's fantasy of Jewish power, as a description of Jewish reality. But Disraeli's imagination of Jewishness did what he needed it to do. It gave him the confidence to compete with the best-born men in England; it gave him the dignity he sustained through the most wounding attacks; it licensed him to see his passage through the world as a noble adventure. Finally, he could say, like Myra at the end of *Endymion*, "All I have desired, all I have dreamed, have come to pass."

As soon as *Endymion* was finished, Disraeli began work on another novel, *Falconet*, but he only had time to finish a few chapters. When the parliamentary session of 1881 opened, despite his frailty, he was in his place in the House of Lords; in March, he had dinner with the queen at Windsor Castle. But later that month, he caught a chill during a snowstorm, and his health began to fail rapidly. The bronchitis that had plagued him for years returned, and he found it harder and harder to breathe. "I feel I am dying," he told a friend. "Whatever the doctors may tell you, I do not believe I shall get well." Early in the morning of April 19, Disraeli briefly emerged from unconsciousness. Sitting up on the bed, he stretched out his arm and moved his lips, as though he were rising to speak in a debate. Ten minutes later, he died. "Just at the moment when his spirit left him," said one watcher by the bedside, "I thought that I had never seen him look so triumphant and full of victory."

FOR FURTHER READING

In writing this book, I have relied constantly on the two major biographies of Benjamin Disraeli, each in its way a masterpiece. *The Life of Benjamin Disraeli, Earl of Beaconsfield*, begun by William Flavelle Monypenny and completed by George Earle Buckle, appeared in six volumes between 1910 and 1920. Running to some two thousand pages, it combines a highly respectful narrative of Disraeli's life with extensive selections from his correspondence, and a practically month-by-month account of parliamentary politics over a period of half a century. All subsequent writers on Disraeli have drawn from Monypenny and Buckle, and a good number of popular biographers do little more than abridge them.

In its authority and comprehensiveness, Monypenny and Buckle's *Life* represents a wonderful late flowering of the nineteenth-century biographical tradition. By the same token, however, it is a decidedly Establishment look at Disraeli, informed by a certain degree of Tory piety, and excessively discreet about matters of sex and money. Robert Blake's *Disraeli*, published in 1966, is the ideal complement and corrective. Blake brings a measured skepticism to Disraeli's legend; he is willing to see improvisation and ambition where Monypenny and Buckle find only high principle.

More broadly, he benefits from a later generation's disabused perspective on the Victorians, while still allowing the reader to appreciate their greatness. Blake's thorough reassessment of Disraeli remains the best starting point for any reader who wants to get to know him.

Of the many other biographies of Disraeli, I found *Young Disraeli: 1804–1846* by Jane Ridley (1995) the most illuminating. While Ridley is sometimes positively unfriendly to her subject, she offers much new detail about the long-buried intrigues of Disraeli's early career. *Disraeli: A Biography* by Stanley Weintraub (1993) stands out for the attention it pays to the Jewish dimension of Disraeli's life and work. Other valuable books focus on specific themes or events in Disraeli's life. *Victoria and Disraeli* by Theo Aronson (1977) is a brief, racy retelling of the relationship between the queen and her favorite prime minister. *Mrs. Dizzy* by Mollie Hardwick (1972), in addition to filling in the usually neglected details of Mary Anne's life, gives a vivid impression of the loose manners of Disraeli's social milieu. *Disraeli, Derby and the Conservative Party: The Political Journals of Lord Stanley, 1849–69*, edited by J. R. Vincent (1978), offers a remarkable behind-the-scenes view of Victorian politics and conveys the fascination that the exotic Disraeli held for an arch-Englishman. *Disraeli, Gladstone, and the Eastern Question* by R. W. Seton-Watson (1935) is a classic study of the diplomatic and political intrigues leading up to the Congress of Berlin, as seen from a decidedly pro-Gladstone perspective. And Robert Blake returned to an important phase of his subject's life in *Disraeli's Grand Tour* (1982), a short study focusing on Disraeli's travels in the East.

In the late nineteenth and early twentieth centuries, publishers on both sides of the Atlantic capitalized on Disraeli's fame by releasing collected editions of his work. When quoting from Disraeli's fiction, my source is usually the twenty-volume "Earl's Edition," published in 1904 with an introduction by Edmund Gosse. This and similar editions are fairly easy to find on the secondhand-book market. Disraeli's most popular novels, *Coningsby* and *Sybil*, are still in print in paperback; for his most important Jewish books, *Alroy* and *Tancred*, facsimile reprints are available. It is a sign of his continuing influence on conservative thought that his political writings have recently been reissued, under the title *Whigs and Whiggism* (2006).

Victorian England has been as extensively written about as any period in history. The relevant volume of the Oxford History of England, *The Age of Reform: 1815–1870* by Sir Llewellyn Woodward (2nd edition, 1962), offers a comprehensive, if dry, introduction to the major issues and events of the period. It is nicely balanced by the rich portrait of *The Victorian World Picture* by David Newsome (1997), which focuses on the way the endlessly articulate and self-conscious Victorians understood themselves. In her collection of essays *Victorian Minds* (1968), Gertrude Himmelfarb looks at some of the main intellectual figures of the age; her essay on the Reform Bill of 1867 powerfully argues that Disraeli's triumph was motivated by conservative principles, not just partisan tactics. *Gladstone: A Biography* by Philip Magnus (1954) is an excellent one-volume life of Disraeli's great antagonist.

For the history of English Jewry, I have mainly relied on *The Jews of Britain, 1656–2000*, by Todd M. Endelman (2002). *The Cousinhood* by Chaim Bermant (1971) is a colorful account of the Anglo-Jewish high society in which Disraeli mingled. The story of the political and legal battle to admit Jews to Parliament is told in great detail in *The Emancipation of the Jews in Britain* by M. C. N. Salbstein (1982). Two major twentieth-century Jewish thinkers have given Disraeli extended treatment in their work: Hannah Arendt devoted a largely hostile section of *The Origins of Totalitarianism* to his Jewish myth-making, while Isaiah Berlin explored the effects of his Jewishness on his politics in the essay "Benjamin Disraeli, Karl Marx and the Search for Identity," in *Against the Current*.

Finally, one of the best books ever written about Disraeli is also one of the earliest: *Lord Beaconsfield*, the 1878 study by the Danish Jewish literary critic Georg Brandes. Relying mainly on his reading of Disraeli's fiction, without the benefit of archival research or private correspondence, Brandes managed to produce an absolutely convincing study of Disraeli's psychology. Later biographers have often done little more than confirm Brandes's intuitions about Disraeli's motives and character. Certainly, no one who spends much time reading and thinking about Disraeli could dissent from Brandes's conclusion: "Almost against my will, a feeling of sympathy took possession of my mind."

CHRONOLOGY

Mid-second
millennium BCE Joseph becomes vizier of Egypt.

c. 1000 BCE King Solomon builds the Temple in Jerusalem.

c. 1027 Shmuel Ha-Nagid becomes vizier of Muslim Granada.

1066 Norman conquest; Norman barons come to England and conquer England from Saxons.

1144 The first blood libel takes place in Norwich, England.

c.1160 David Alroy, a Kurdish Jew, leads rebellion against Seljuk Turks in Azerbaijan.

1190 King Richard I brings the crusading spirit to England; Jews are massacred around the country.

1290 King Edward I expels the Jews from England.

Chronology

1492   Expulsion of the Jews from Spain. Isaac Aboab, a leader of the Jewish community in Castile, negotiates with the king of Portugal to allow some Spanish Jews to move to Portugal.

1497   King Manuel I of Portugal declares that all Jews must convert to Christianity.

1616   Uriel da Costa, a Portuguese Jew living in Amsterdam, composes his Eleven Theses, rejecting rabbinic Judaism. He is repeatedly expelled from the Jewish community.

1656   Oliver Cromwell, motivated by a desire to disperse the Jews throughout the globe in order to hasten the "Second Coming," unofficially encourages Manasseh ben Israel, a rabbi of the Sephardic community in Amsterdam, to reestablish a Jewish community in England.

1688   Glorious Revolution establishes that Parliament, not the monarch, has supreme power in Britain.

1748   Benjamin D'Israeli comes to England from Italy at the age of eighteen.

1766   Birth of son, Isaac, to Benjamin D'Israeli and his wife, Sarah.

1780   Moses Mendelssohn, a Jewish philosopher, publishes *Jerusalem*, in which he asserts that Jews should have a right to civic participation.

1791 Isaac D'Israeli publishes *Curiosities of Literature*, an instant bestseller.

1802 Isaac D'Israeli marries Maria Basevi, from a Spanish family descended from Isaac Aboab, the last Gaon of Castile.

December 21, 1804 Birth of son, Benjamin, to Isaac and Maria D'Israeli.

1813 Isaac D'Israeli invited to serve as *parnass* of Bevis Marks Synagogue in London; he refuses.

1815 England's final defeat of Napoléon.

1817 D'Israeli children Sarah, Benjamin, Ralph, and James are baptized in the Church of England.

Benjamin sent to Higham Hall, a small school run by a Unitarian minister.

1821 Benjamin begins training to become an attorney.

1823 Benjamin changes name from D'Israeli to Disraeli.

July 1824 Benjamin leaves law firm, tours Germany with his father, then begins to invest in South American mining interests.

1824 Death of Lord Byron, the English Romantic poet.

Summer 1825 Disraeli, with publisher John Murray, attempts to launch new liberal newspaper, the *Representative;* paper is short-lived and Disraeli's involvement ends quickly.

1825 Robert Plumer Ward publishes *Tremaine, or the Man of Refinement*, the first work of fiction to accurately describe high-society life.

The German Jewish poet and writer Heinrich Heine converts to Lutheranism in order to improve his career options; he soon regrets his conversion and tries to return to the Jewish community.

1826 Disraeli anonymously publishes *Vivian Grey*, a novel of a young man of great ambition; the book's readers are disappointed to discover that the author is not actually a member of high society and Disraeli falls into deep depression.

1828 Disraeli publishes *Popanilla*, a short satire.

May 1830 Disraeli, with brother-in-law-to-be William Meredith and later joined by friend James Clay, begins traveling the Mediterranean.

1830 Revolution in France replaces Bourbon dynasty with constitutional monarchy.

November 1830 Whig party comes to power in England, with mandate for Reform Bill.

February 1831 Disraeli visits Jerusalem.

July 1831 William Meredith dies of smallpox in Cairo; Disraeli returns to England.

1831 Disraeli publishes *The Young Duke.*

May 1832 Disraeli publishes *Contarini Fleming.*

June 1832 King William IV pushes passage of Reform Bill, beginning of extension of suffrage in England among British landholders.

Disraeli runs for Parliament in High Wycombe as a "high Radical"; he is defeated by Charles Grey, the son of the Prime Minister; runs again in December and is again defeated.

1832 Gladstone enters parliament at the age of twenty-two.

1833 Disraeli publishes *The Wondrous Tale of Alroy.*

Isaac D'Israeli publishes *The Genius of Judaism.*

1835 Disraeli stands for Parliament in Taunton as Tory candidate and is again defeated. Challenges Irish Catholic leader Daniel O'Connell to a duel.

1836 Disraeli publishes *Henrietta Temple*, the title of which was inspired by his then-mistress, Henrietta Sykes, whom he had met in 1833.

1837 Disraeli publishes *Venetia*.

Moses Montefiore elected Sheriff of London.

June 1837 Death of King William IV leads to ascension of Queen Victoria and calling of new elections.

July 1837 Disraeli elected to Parliament from the borough of Maidstone.

1838–42 Chartist Movement in England demands universal male suffrage.

1839 Disraeli marries Mary Anne Lewis, widow of his fellow Maidstone MP.

1840 The Damascus affair, in which prominent Syrian Jews are accused of the ritual murder of an Italian monk in Damascus; Jews from Western Europe, including Moses Montefiore, eventually intervene and save the lives of several of the accused.

1841 Conservative Party comes to power in Parliament; Disraeli is elected MP for Shrewsbury.

1844 Disraeli publishes *Coningsby*.

1845 Disraeli publishes *Sybil*.

Friedrich Engels publishes *The Condition of the Working Class in England*.

1846 The battle over the repeal of the Corn Laws brings down Prime Minister Sir Robert Peel, elevates Disraeli to a leading role in the weakened Conservative Party.

1847 Disraeli publishes *Tancred*.

April 1847 Death of Disraeli's mother, Maria.

1847 Lionel de Rothschild elected to the House of Commons but cannot take seat because of oath on "the true faith of a Christian"; Disraeli reelected, representing Buckinghamshire.

December 1847 Liberal Prime Minister Lord John Russell introduces bill to exempt Jews from taking oath "on the true faith of a Christian" to enter Parliament. Disraeli supports the bill, at the risk of alienating his Tory supporters.

January 1848 Death of Disraeli's father, Isaac.

Late 1848 Disraeli purchases Hughenden, an estate near High Wycombe.

1851 Disraeli publishes a biography of Lord George Bentick, his late Tory colleague.

Disraeli is befriended by Mrs. Brydges Willyams, née Sarah Mendez da Costa, an elderly convert from Judaism who becomes his confidante.

1852 Disraeli serves briefly as Chancellor of the Exchequer in the First Derby Administration when a split between Whigs and Peelites enables the Tories to form a government.

1854–56 The Crimean War pits Britain, France, and Turkey against Russia.

1857 The Indian Mutiny shakes Britain's hold on its most important colony.

1858 Members of the House of Commons no longer required to swear oath including the words "the true faith of a Christian."

February 1858 Disraeli again serves as Chancellor of the Exchequer under Lord Derby when Conservatives, once more, come to power for a brief period.

1859 Darwin publishes *The Origin of Species.*

Death of Disraeli's sister Sarah.

1861   Death of Prince Albert, consort of Queen
Victoria. Disraeli's letters of consolation
to the Queen open a new period of intimacy between them.

1862   The German socialist Moses Hess publishes *Rome and Jerusalem*, in which he
makes a case for Zionism and for Jewishness as a racial identity.

1863   Mrs. Brydges Willyams dies, leaving
Disraeli her fortune.

October 1865   Prime Minister Lord Palmerston dies;
Lord John Russell takes his place at the
head of the Liberal government.

June 1866   The Conservative Party defeats the
Liberal Party's Reform Bill to extend the
franchise by four hundred thousand
voters; Liberal government resigns and
Conservatives return to power under
Lord Derby.

August 1867   Disraeli, as Leader of the Conservative
Party in the House of Commons, suc-
ceeds in passing the Second Reform Bill,
which gives the right to vote to most
male heads of households.

February 27, 1868   Disraeli becomes Prime Minister of a
minority government.

Chronology

November 1868 Gladstone and Liberal Party win decisive victory in Parliament.

1870 Disraeli publishes *Lothair*.

December 1872 Death of Disraeli's wife, Mary Anne.

February 1874 Disraeli becomes Prime Minister in a Conservative landslide. His government carries out his campaign promise to pass new social welfare legislation.

November 1875 Disraeli arranges for England to buy shares in the Suez Canal Company using funds borrowed from the Rothschilds.

1876 George Eliot publishes *Daniel Deronda*, a proto-Zionist novel with a sympathetic Jewish protagonist.

Anthony Trollope publishes *The Prime Minister*, a novel with a Jewish villain.

Disraeli introduces Royal Titles Bill, to add the title Empress of India to Queen Victoria's title.

May 1876 Massacre of Bulgarian Christians by Muslim Turkish soldiers, leading to instability in the Ottoman Empire and threatening Britain's foreign policy.

August 12, 1876 Disraeli is created Earl of Beaconsfield; leads Government from the House of Lords.

April 1877 Russia declares war on Turkey.

March 1878 Treaty of San Stefano ends the war between Russia and Turkey, creates Bulgaria, gives Russia significant territory in Asia Minor.

April 1878 Disraeli orders troops from India to the Mediterranean to be in place for possible war with Russia.

June 1878 The Congress of Berlin brings together statesman from all over Europe to negotiate the future of the Balkans; Bulgarian territory is redrawn, and Britain gains control over Cyprus. Disraeli is recognized as the star of the Congress.

November 1878 British viceroy in India, Lord Lytton, launches Second Afghan War.

January 1879 British troops defeated in Zulu War.

April 1880 Conservative Party is defeated; Disraeli leaves office.

September 1880 Disraeli completes his final novel *Endymion*.

April 19, 1881   Disraeli dies.

1882   Russia's oppressive May Laws and state-sponsored pogroms lead tens of thousands of Jews to immigrate to England and America.

1885   Nathaniel de Rothschild, son of Lionel, becomes the first Jewish member of the House of Lords.

1896   Theodore Herzl publishes *The Jewish State.*

1897   First Zionist Congress in Basel.

1917   British conquer the land of Israel from the Ottoman Empire.

November 2, 1917   The British government issues the Balfour Declaration promising "The Establishment in Palestine of a national home for the Jewish people."

May 14, 1948   State of Israel is founded.

ABOUT THE AUTHOR

Adam Kirsch, a book critic for *The New York Sun*, is the author of two collections of poetry, *Invasions* and *The Thousand Wells*, as well as *The Wounded Surgeon: Confession and Transformation in Six American Poets* and *The Modern Element: Essays on Contemporary Poetry*.